T0021601

Subaltern Studies 2.0

Subaltern Studies 2.0

Being against the Capitalocene

Milinda Banerjee

Jelle J.P. Wouters

with

Gayatri Chakravorty Spivak

Marisol de la Cadena

Thom van Dooren

Suraj Yengde

PRICKLY
PARADIGM
PRESS

©2022 by the authors. All rights reserved.

Prickly Paradigm Press, LLC
5751 S. Woodlawn Ave.
Chicago, IL 60637

www.prickly-paradigm.com

ISBN: 9781734643534
Library of Congress Control Number: 2022944946

Artwork credits:
Frontispiece and page 86 by Pema Gyeltshen
Page 74 by Senganglu Thaimei

Printed in the United States of America on acid-free paper.

Table of Contents

The Constitution of the Cosmos

Exhortations

Who Speaks?

In the history of humanity, the author is a recent invention—
Usurpation of community by private ownership.

It is speech that speaks in community:
Gods, muses, ancestors, winds, spirits of animals and trees,
      rivers, humans in assembly.
Speech speaks in assembly:
Bards and minstrels convey to the assembly its own
      consciousness,
Make audible what it already knows.

This pamphlet is assembly—
Indra's net,
Where every being sees and reflects every other.
Naga elders, Bhutanese herders and yaks, Greek and Roman
      seers, Indian poets,

Revolutionaries, feminists, ecological intellectuals, cranes,
   fungi,
Even theorists of state and capital we unyoke ourselves from,
Take their place in this assembly.
Words gather.

We thank Naga, Bhutanese, and other South Asian
   communities
Who haunt our being.
We acclaim their wisdom carriers
Past, present, in advent.

We acknowledge their friends and kin—
Human, animal, vegetal
Fungal, numinous, elemental.
We acknowledge and acclaim other rooted communities
From Amazonia to Zomia,
Whose wisdom we consulted through scholarship by and
   about them.
Their norm worlds—
Desecrated by state and capital—
Vivifying struggle, survivance, continuance.

This pamphlet refuses author authority—
Expanding beyond individual positionality
We learn and relate.

Relationality is assembly
Chariot of the sun
An unresting wheel.

We see ourselves less as author-owners of words
And more as bards singing about a war.
Our words are common—
Battlefield din.

Speech arouses beings
Leads them in chorus.
Being sings of Being
Truth roars.

War of Unbeing against Being

State and capital haunt the world today. Our desire for security and power becomes an alien force and rules us as the state. Our desire for possessions becomes an alien power and rules us as capital. We are imprisoned by our desires, which rule us beings as alien Unbeing. The state feeds on our fear; capital preys on our greed. This pamphlet outlines some thoughts we can commonly share to overcome state and capital, and revitalize Being. Being is that which makes beings beings—that which connects them—what makes life possible—that which is. Being shines in beings—in the relations that weave them together.

Humans with power coerce fellow human and non-human beings to work for corporations—legal persons, artificial beings, mortal gods. State and capital depend on unequal exchange. The state promises protection in return for our taxes and obedience. Capital promises pleasure and profit, and rules through addiction, fostering desires, and robbing the earth and its denizens to fuel accumulation, an empire of growth without limits. State and capital take more than they give; the interdependence of Being requires that we give more than we take.

We draw from the Subaltern Studies tradition the central insight that community offers our best chance to resist state and capital. The tradition was born from the tide of Indian anti-imperialism and decolonization. The decline of Subaltern Studies in the late 1990s stemmed from the triumph of neoliberal capital, sanctioned by right-wing nationalism. In the India of Rajiv Gandhi and P. V. Narasimha Rao, as in Margaret Thatcher's Britain and Ronald Reagan's United States, neoliberal policies gradually dismantled welfarist programs of redistributing wealth and opportunity to subaltern actors. The demise of the Soviet Union eroded the plausibility of a future beyond capitalism.

Today the tide has begun to turn again. From Buenos Aires to Whanganui, voices are rising against the condominium of violent state and neoliberal capital. The time has come to ally these voices ascending from Indigenous societies, Black congregations, Dalit-Bahujan public spheres, antiextractivist and antiextinction struggles, queer communities, feminist strikes. One link at a time—one mountain, one river, one forest, one injured species, one plant community, one vulnerable minority at a time—we shall reverse the chains of subject- and commodity making, of de-souling, that have precipitated the Great Unbeing. Niyamgiri,

Whanganui, and Black Lives Matter embody political ontologies where beings are affirmed as beings. To borrow words from the Black theologian M. Shawn Copeland, they embody "a cry of presence." This is a long revolution, rather than the messianic overcoming that the twentieth century reposed faith in. There is no time to despair.

The time is ripe for a revitalization of Subaltern Studies, four decades since the birth of the tradition. Where Subaltern Studies 1.0 focused on local communities in India, Subaltern Studies 2.0 must offer pathways for heterogeneous social coalitions that ally resistant communities across the world. Where Subaltern Studies 1.0 focused on human communities, we must recognize the interdependence between human and nonhuman that has always characterized noncapitalist life worlds: think through multibeing communities.

Truth is unforgetting, reversing the great oblivion that has made us forget what our ancestors knew—that humans and other-than-humans together inhabit Being, and can be separated only at the cost of perdition. Hence, the new Subaltern Studies, like the old one, must ally history and anthropology. Anthropology helps history to harness the treasure trove of cultural traditions that it lethargically watches over but is unable to politicize. It persuades history to allocate equal value to the "philosophies without philosophers" that anthropologists have written about, and to take seriously other-than-human beings as subjects of intellection.

A New Anticolonial Struggle

Decolonization has only been half done. In India—and surely elsewhere too—anticolonial politics was often anarchist, seeking to overthrow the European-colonial state-capital nexus, rather than preserve it. The postcolonial state was a betrayal, more than a realization, of many anticolonial dreams. To complete decolonization, the modern sovereign state form—colonial origin across large stretches of Asia, Africa, and the Americas—needs to be dismantled. Contemporary capitalist value extraction draws upon racial-colonial as well as older precolonial hierarchies. Decolonization should involve the dismantling of capital. The time has come for a new anticolonial struggle.

From Dakota to Niyamgiri, a new freedom struggle has already begun. Our prime task is to support it. Subaltern Studies 2.0 must offer pathways to overcome state and capital. It will express and ally voices that have already emerged, articulate what the world has already realized in its inner core. Against the rootlessness of capital, it posits a vision of rooted interdependence: rooted communities, past and present, that span and connect with each other, like symbiotic arboreal roots and fungi that nourish and protect each other. These symbioses help the communities to dissolve the hierarchies and exclusions that are internal to them; in working together, each becomes more equal internally, as does the common world.

Political commentators are preoccupied today with building a new apparatus of revolution: theorizing about new assemblies, new parties, new policies, to replace the failed god of the Communist Party. (We all write in the shadow of the fall of the Soviet Union and the transformation beyond recognition of China.) They offer important insights, some discussed in detail below. But their principal weakness is that they do not center-stage the revolutionary communities that already exist, that have existed for centuries in the non-Western world, that have periodically overthrown empires, that have survived and ravaged colonial states and their postcolonial epigoni. We shall not reinvent the wheel, announce a new organization of revolution. We enunciate to the world the potential it already has: these communities that already exist and must ally to overthrow the superstratum of state and capital.

> All the stars of the night are there
> In the depths of the light of day.
> —Rabindranath Tagore, "Hathat Dekha"

The Age of Sorrow

The accumulation of power and property alike requires that beings be treated not as beings but as living corpses: vocal and nonvocal instruments to be subjected, used, consumed. The commodity is the corpse of Being; the subject is commodity with half a will still left. The world is food for state and capital. Hence the Age of Capital is the Age of Sorrow. The World Health Organization notes that more than 264 million people are affected by depression today. Further, "there has been a 13% rise in mental health conditions and substance use disorders in the last decade (to 2017). Mental health conditions now cause 1 in 5 years lived with disability."

William Cowper's description of "The Solitude of Alexander Selkirk" summarizes man under capitalism: "monarch of all I survey [...] lord of the fowl and the brute," but resigned to sovereign loneliness. Happiness arises from interdependence; it erodes as community shrinks and greed becomes king. Joy is social camaraderie. For those subalternized due to their class, gender, and ethnicity, the toll is higher: an overwhelming despair at lack of agency.

Here, as elsewhere, the COVID-19 pandemic has exposed the callousness of ruling classes and deficits of privatized health care, from the United States to Brazil and India. Photographs from India of rivers awash with corpses and undying funeral pyres bring to mind end times. Rich countries have created an oligopoly over the global vaccine supply, buying more than they need, with little thought for poorer countries. Tedros Adhanom Ghebreyesus, Director General of WHO, wrote in April 2021 that "of the more than 890 million vaccine doses that have been administered globally, more than 81 percent have been given in high- and upper-middle-income countries. Low-income countries have received just 0.3 percent." Discussions about doing away with vaccine patents have run across repeated shibboleths about the sanctity of corporate property. Arguing against patent waivers, German Chancellor Angela Merkel suggests that "we need the creativity and the power of innovation of companies, and to me, that includes patent protection."

The mood of global despair is captured by a line in the Bengali musician Anupam Roy's recent hit song "Manush bhalo nei": "human beings are not well." Living in another era of state formation, commercialization, and increasing inequality—similar to ours in terms of breakdown of community life—the Buddha had diagnosed *dukkha*, suffering, as the human condition, fueled by *tanha*, thirst. Desire, the thirst for possession, ignites both state and capital, fueling an economy of suffering. Capital is death.

The Evil Twins: Sovereignty and Property

The binary between sovereignty and property, state and economic corporation, conceals their commonality, their *achintyabhedabheda*, unthinkable difference and nondifference. The Shanti Parva of the Sanskrit epic *Mahabharata* (late first millennium BCE) presents an original condition when there was neither state nor ruler. Beings protected each other through righteousness. The fall happened when they became subject to greed, *lobha*, and righteousness was lost. Kingship arose to mediate this disorder. The state allowed human beings to say *mamedam*, this is mine. The logic in this ancient text is clear: covetousness gives rise to conflict and paves the way for the state, which legitimates possessiveness as law. "This is mine" is the possessive will: my territory, my state, my property, against yours. Beings—humans, cattle, birds, forests, fish—are now violently abstracted into commodities: they become subjects and possessions.

In Hegel's *Phenomenology of Spirit*, when two beings encounter each other, they fight until one, terrified to its inmost being—in mortal fear of "death, the absolute master"—becomes the *Knecht*/bondsman and the other the *Herr*/lord. The bondsman works; his labor produces for the lord what the latter shall consume. It is possible to see here the founding moment of both state and possession. James Scott puts this in another way in *Against the Grain* when he says that the state is born when humans domesticate other humans, as they once domesticated plants and animals.

The possessive will animates these acts of subjecting. In *Philosophy of Right*, Hegel identifies the will at the birth moment of both the sovereign state and property. The ruler says, "I will," just as every property owner asserts his will on what he claims to be his possessions. Violence animates the exercise of sovereignty as well as processes of production and consumption—expropriating people to get their lands; felling trees; slaughtering animals; catching fish; suppressing workers' struggles for better wages. Violence is necessary and inevitable in distinguishing mine and yours: in transforming beings into subjects to be ruled; into labor, resources, and energy to be extracted for profit. The realm of commodity production and exchange is an everyday slaughterhouse no less than the battlefield. The factory is a miniature dictatorship.

In *The Concept of the Political*, Carl Schmitt distinguished between the political and the economic—between the sphere of sovereign friendship and enmity and the sphere of competitive profit making—though he also confessed to overlaps between the two domains. The distinction carries even less weight today than in Schmitt's time. Capitalist production and exchange have ensnared all life. They trap everyone in a web of commodity and money; alienate everything to a regime of quantified material value; put a price on every head. Capital subsumes sovereignty. Earlier debates on whether capitalism would undermine, sustain, or reinvent state sovereignty have run their course. At the turn of the millennium, Michael Hardt and Antonio

Negri were premature when they predicted in *Empire* that capitalist globalization would precipitate the decline of nation-state sovereignty. Instead, state and capital have grown symbiotic for mutual profit, fusing patriotism with production, nationalism with resource extraction. Refusal to contribute to the numbers that are made to stand for economic growth is now construed as sedition, as Adivasis in India and Amazonians in Brazil have discovered.

Today, Gross Domestic Product (GDP)—called by its historian, Philipp Lepenies, "the most powerful statistical figure in human history"—orders society. During the Second World War, the United States emphasized Gross National Product (GNP) calculation as a metric of national strength. Subsequently, the Western bloc fetishized the calculation of economic growth to fight against Soviet communism and suppress popular demands for wealth redistribution. Under neoliberalism, GDP symbolizes life denuded by capital—Being abstracted to pure monetary value. The figure of the patriot is no longer solely one who is willing to sacrifice their life for the nation but also one who produces and consumes plentifully, fueling national economic growth. Indian nationalist politicians emphasize "Make in India" and persuade Indians to boycott Chinese products; for American nationalists, "America First" must translate into production and consumption choices as well. The nation is commodified as a brand.

The symbiosis of capital and state has dissolved the boundaries between politicians and CEOs. The Brazilian state facilitates capitalist primitive accumulation at the expense of the Amazon rainforest and its Indigenous denizens. In India, the Hindu nationalist government aligns the unification of the country under Hindu religion with the unification of a national market under oligarchic corporations. Muslim, Dalit, and Adivasi-Indigenous bodies are reduced to bare lives, steady supplies of cheap labor under high-caste control. Aggressively nationalist China enshrines in the constitution of the Communist Party the world's largest capitalist experiment in the form of the Belt and Road Initiative. If successful, this New Silk Road, as a joint venture between state and capital, may witness China's definitive jump to transnational hegemony, making it a global superproprietor of the sovereign "I will."

The Subjection of Being

But, how did this possessive will—the sensibility of "this is mine," "I will"—arise in the first place? In his essay "The Original Political Society," the anthropologist Marshall Sahlins observed that originally gods—and other godlike beings, such as ancestors—were seen as wielders of political and economic power. They were the true sovereigns and owners. Such structures of possession are still visible in many relatively egalitarian, if not classless societies, as among the Inuits, in Indigenous Amazonia and Zomia, and in Aboriginal Australia. However, in many regions of the world, some human beings gradually usurped this position. They took the place of the gods to emerge as sovereigns, producing the state.

This human usurpation of the divine is generally cast as the opposite: a generous gift of the gods/God to chosen humans. In Virgil's *Aeneid*, Jupiter, king of the gods, gives "empire without end" to the Romans. This empire has "neither boundaries of things nor times." White settler colonialism, in the Lockean mode, derives justification from God's gifting of the world to Adam and his worthy—industrious, rational, white, male—successors. In John Locke's language, "God, by commanding to subdue, gave Authority so far to *appropriate*." Caliphates claim divine sanction in conquering lands and enslaving infidels. It is hardly surprising that in his lord-bondsman dialectic, Hegel quotes the Bible—"the fear of the Lord is the beginning of wisdom"—which puts beings to work for the master. To question this terrorizing lordship, which structures both sovereignty and property today, we need to go beyond Sahlins and identify a more primal usurpation: the usurpation of Being by the gods themselves.

In early India, as state formation and the spread of elite property eroded the commons, the *Brihadaranyaka Upanishad* (seventh to sixth century BCE) registered its protest against this possessive will. As humans want to own livestock, it argues, so do the gods want to own humans. The gods do not want humans to be free. However, beings who realize their identity with all other beings free themselves from this servitude. To use modern language, it is only false consciousness that keeps us unfree. Servitude thrives when we cannot see the identity and equality of all beings, when we think some to be superior and others to be their possessions.

These then are the steps of subjection. In the first step, Being is heterogenized, and the gods/God are cast as sovereign owners of other beings. This is religion, this is the founding of sovereignty. (Robert Yelle argues in *Sovereignty and the Sacred* that religion is just sovereignty under another name.) In later steps, some men claim divine sanction to assert ownership over other beings, thereby constructing sovereignty and property.

Once When There Was No State, No Capital

This ascendancy of state sovereignty and private property implied the diminution of the much wider spectrum of ways through which human beings had earlier related to each other as well as to nonhuman beings. Marcel Mauss famously showed how devotion to individualized private property—and the related obsession with using exchange exclusively to accumulate monetary profit—was rejected by many so-called "archaic societies." They rejected the alienation between people and objects that constructs the impersonality of capitalist commodity exchange. Instead they developed "gift economies" arranged around three obligations: to give, to receive, and to reciprocate. The purpose was to make mutual relations, not simply profit. These societies often denounced exchanges that were calibrated by pure commercial calculation.

Many "archaic societies" devised elaborate techniques to prevent the consolidation of anything like private property, centered on a singular man claiming "This is mine." Richard Lee and others have shown how the few material possessions of the Kalahari hunter-gatherers constantly circled among group members. None could claim them as their private property, and all went to great lengths to share objects, food, and water with other members of the band. In a harsh environment, sharing meant the spreading of risks and enhanced chances of collective survival. Private property would induce jealousy and thus divide the community, making everyone more vulnerable to the famines and droughts. Men continually deprecated each other's hunting achievements. The intention was to preclude the hunter, whose kill was eaten communally, from thinking of himself as a chief or provider and of others as his inferiors.

Even when social hierarchies had congealed irreversibly, societies often evolved mechanisms for negating the accumulation of surplus—preventing surplus from transforming into profit-seeking capital. Among the Naga in the Indo-Burma borderland, the village rich had to absolve their wealth through communal feasts of merit. The community reciprocated with embroidered shawls, house carvings, and the erection of monoliths in the feast giver's name. In this prestige economy, generosity, not accumulation, mediated social standing. In this light, we can also better understand the great potlatches of the Pacific Northwest coast. These involved the deliberate giving away or destroying of wealth in order to establish a leader's power. Sacrificing the possibility of capital was the necessary precondition for winning power and status. Competitive gifting by big men served a comparable purpose in Melanesia. In all cases, relational value was privileged over abstract exchange value. Status arose from the limitation of capital. Exchange between social beings subsumed and overrode exchange of reified commodities.

Yet other communities rejected state sovereignty altogether. The earlier social-evolutionary assumption had been that stateless societies had not yet developed the level of civilization essential to have states. Pierre Clastres asked: But what if the Amazonians were quite aware of what the elementary form of state organization might be like; what it might mean to live under its structures of command and obedience, and for that very reason had purposefully organized their societies to prevent the state from growing inside them? Similarly, James Scott questioned: What if the Zomians in highland Asia were not so much left behind by state civilization but had sought to escape its oppressive power by seeking refuge in the hills, accepting poverty as the necessary price of freedom? In these societies, the contagion of state-capital that had evolved in neighboring regions, whether among the Incas or the Thais, had been comprehensively and consciously rejected for millennia.

What can we learn from these societies? Let us consider the Nagas in the Indo-Burma borderland. They persistently resisted the arrival in their hills of Ahom, Manipuri, British, Burmese, Japanese, and Indian valley-states. They also prevented statelike forms from emerging organically. At the heart of this was a tenacious localism. The Naga village owned the means of production, and labor was arranged communally within the village. Language varied from village to village, and often across *khels* (wards) within the same village. There was no uniform grammar, script, epic, or song that would transcend village frontiers and connect multiple localities.

Like labor-force and word-force, soul-force (*aren*, in Ao Naga) also accumulated at the village level. Nagas believed this to be responsible for the flourishing of crops, cattle, and children. They felt that it needed to be periodically replenished—the source was decapitated heads of enemies. Hence Nagas celebrated warriors who brought back enemy heads, reserving manhood and marriage for them. Enemy heads were welcomed with ritual fanfare and hung from village gates or fixed on poles by the side of the path leading to the fields, so that their soul matter entered the village and fields. Relatedly, Nagas upheld physical strength, courage, and boldness as cardinal values.

Empires in the Indian plains—from the Mauryas to the Mughals and the British—continually waged war and slaughtered enemies. States close to the Naga highlands, such as the Ahom and the Jaintia polities, performed regular human sacrifices. For example, around 1400 CE, the Ahom ruler invited a large number of Nagas for a lavish feast, only to murder them and publicly exhibit their heads. (The *mundamala*, garland of heads, was an Ahom method of dealing with enemies of the state.) Such examples may well have made the Nagas fearful of the state form. They may have felt that states needed to be resisted because they would collect Naga heads on a much more massive scale than anything the Nagas accomplished.

Unlike state warfare, Naga headhunting remained local in scale. The depletion of manpower through internecine conflict prevented the formation of a centralized polity that would accumulate the manpower and transform it into a state. Headhunting quite literally kept the Nagas politically acephalous. In fact, the soul matter of clan and village leaders was deemed to be particularly fertile and sought after. As these leaders were periodically decapitated, we might, with a pinch of salt, call the Nagas a society of the guillotine. The British Raj and the postcolonial Indian state, although they formally abolished headhunting, consolidated their rule through the violent sacrifice of many more Naga lives than had been required by the nonstate economy of soul force.

It should be clear that while the Nagas can instruct us about the benefits of keeping labor, culture, and politics radically decentralized, one of the ways they achieved this—through headhunting—is not a pathway we would prescribe to our readers. We can learn radical democracy from the Nagas in the same way we can be inspired by the French Revolution without admiring the Reign of Terror. Our relation to the societies we learn our pathways from is dialectical, not nostalgic.

The Monstrosity of State and Capital

State societies follow a different grammar of power, based on continuous accumulation and centralization of authority. To draw on Michel Foucault, here humans successfully claim to be shepherds of other humans. Hammurabi, king of Babylon, described himself as the benevolent shepherd of his people; in Sanskritic India, the ruler was often called *gopa/gopati*, the herdsman; the modern European state inherited from the church many of its pastoral responsibilities. Quintessentially, state power is pastoral power, the power to domesticate and own the flock—indissociably bound with the power to extract the labor of the flock and exchange the resulting commodities.

When humans extract labor and energy from beings, trade in the fruits of their work without care for their weal, they transform beings into commodities. This is the source of material accumulation in its many names and forms: tax, rent, and profit. Accumulated capital is harnessed to put yet more beings to work and extract yet more from the earth—capital as master is the sovereign lord of beings. As Marx observed in *Capital*, capital is dead labor that feeds like a vampire on living beings. Sovereignty and property are necromancy.

Accumulation of capital proceeds through the draining and murder of being: through putting dying being to work. In Edwin Ardener's report, the Bakweri in Cameroon understood that capitalist accumulation necessitated turning the living into the "living dead" through witchcraft. These undead provided bonded labor to avaricious witch masters. Capital removed the soul from humans; desouled labourers produced soulless commodities. Capital was king of zombies; capitalism was soul stealing. Among the Khasis of northeast India, capital accumulation often involved deals with a demon who offered instant wealth. In return, the humans had to sacrifice their relatives to the demon, often represented as a vampire snake. Capital accumulation took shape as a snake that drained human life and blood.

Among South American peasants, acquisition of money necessitated the bartering of souls through the devil pact. As the title of Michael Taussig's book *The Devil and Commodity Fetishism in South America* indicates, this devil pact embodied capitalist exchange. Where an earlier society of peasant production had been based on social relations and use value, the capitalist economy was grounded in exchange value. The alienation of human life and labor was central to the exchange of commodities and money; it fueled the growth of surplus value or profit. Indigenous communities understood earlier than many Western theorists that capitalist accumulation is constant necropolitics. It requires some beings to die so that others may accumulate wealth. Capital subsumes life and labor in a cosmic theater of sacrifice, a relentless vampirical ontophagy.

Since the sixteenth century, the corporation has emerged as the prime form through which regimes of sovereignty and capital accumulation have gradually conquered the planet. The English East India Company, the Dutch East India Company (VOC), the Royal Niger Company, and the United Fruit Company were, of course, archetypal company-states. They exemplify how the state form and the company form have been enmeshed with each other in this world-historical march of subjugating nonwhite peoples, from Asia to Africa and Latin America. Philip Stern sees corporate sovereignty as the generic form of which the modern state and the modern company constitute overlapping subtypes.

These artificial persons, these legal beings, did not exactly invent sovereignty or property, but they concentrated political-military power and sharpened labor and resource extraction to a hitherto unprecedented degree. Acephalous and polycentric polities with relatively egalitarian class relations had subsisted until the last few centuries in many parts of the world, including the Americas, Australia, Africa, and parts of South and Southeast Asia. These societies were now subjected to more centralized and exploitative governments.

Capital Colonizes Being

"Capitalism" is the term best used to label this trajectory that generalizes the commodification of beings, turning the earth into a reservoir of resources for profit, decimating resistance. Capitalism is the generalization of the commodity form: everything is now available for sale and purchase. It is the generalization of the value form: everything carries a monetary value and is equivalent in the marketplace of exchange. Capital makes all equal, so that profit is accumulated through production and exchange—ever-expanding profit fueling the empire without limits of capital, with no boundaries of things or time. Capital becomes its own justification. Moishe Postone rightly observes that this creates a relativism of substantive ends. Where profit making is the ultimate reason for being, everything else can have only a relative and provisional moral value.

Capital colonizes life. Ancestry tests extract our DNA to sell us our supposed identity. Big Pharma patents genes and even living organisms; cells and other body parts are routinely traded. Hilary and Steven Rose warn about the ensuing dangers of consumer eugenics and of the commodification of bioinformation. Mental behavior is pathologized to market drugs and psychiatric treatment. Capital thus commodifies the mind and draws the boundary between reason and unreason. In relation to the marketing of antidepressant drugs,

Stefan Ecks speaks about a new form of pharmaceutical citizenship. Capitalist reason seeks to socially exile those who would not meet the demands of the mental health industry. There is no place for the inspired madman, the holy fool, in the city of capital.

Capital transforms our online behavior on platforms like Google and Facebook into commodities. Big Tech corporations steal value from our experiences and emotions, selling data about our online behavior to other companies. Machine intelligence enables advertising that manipulates our desires in order to sell us products. Political parties buy our data to win elections, as the recent Facebook–Cambridge Analytica scandal revealed. Parties that command greater capital can win more easily; information is tribute.

Privacy is a mirage in this world. Choice is a commodity—as well as informational raw material that states use to keep track of, control, and increasingly punish our politics. Shoshana Zuboff calls this "surveillance capitalism." From the United States to China and India, our bodies and minds are subjects of state policing and corporate manipulation. Google CEO Sundar Pichai speaks about every user having "their own individual Google." Zuboff notes that this also implies that Google has every individual. In capitalism, we are possessed by our possessions, commodified by our cravings. Google and Facebook create individualized worlds for us; ensnared, we allow corporations endless profit from our desires.

This is the equality where all life is equally degraded. This is the liberty where our desires trap and own our souls. In capitalism, beings are generalized into things to be produced, objects to be consumed. Labor of humans and nonhumans is alike a commodity: we are all bondsmen to King Capital. Hence, in its broad-minded generosity, capitalism can accept myriad forms of politics, from monarchy and dictatorship to liberal democracy and the social-welfare state. It can acknowledge diverse social relations, from slavery and bonded labor to nominally free wage labor. It only does not brook any resistance to the general drive to commodify everything and all beings for the pursuit of profit, that is, for its own expansion: to expropriate humans of their lands and communities, to atomize them, to destroy the earth, to annihilate entire civilizations and cosmologies that have survived millennia—so that, as in the prophecy of *The Communist Manifesto*, all that is solid melts into air.

The Age of Death

The same hand that transforms beings into resources and invents nature as a presence without living presences ensures that the environment is born stunted and degraded, hurtling into a future of extinction of species, degradation of land and water, pollution of the air, and warming of the globe. Andreas Malm shows how British colonial capitalism fueled the coal industry, accelerated greenhouse gas emissions, and precipitated global warming. Jason Moore castigates the Capitalocene, the age when the world is trapped in the web of capital.

Justin McBrien calls our era the Necrocene. King Capital presides over the sixth mass extinction. Vampire fuel—coal and oil—powers this age of death. Jason Hickel notes that the rate of extinction is now a thousand times higher than prior to the Industrial Revolution. The World Wide Fund for Nature (WWF) Living Planet Report 2018 reveals that 60 percent of the wildlife population of the world decreased just between 1970 and 2014 due to habitat loss, overhunting, overfishing, and similar human activities, generally fueled by commerce. The possessive will that exploits and exhausts human labor also evacuates the earth, and—if left unresisted—ultimately depletes life and extinguishes Being itself.

> This is a strange time.
> When nothing remains strange anymore.
> When no one knows

If water remains in the river or not.

When no one knows

If clouds remain on the mountains or not.

Grandfather, I live in a strange time.

When there is no light in the sky,

When there is no light in the soil,

When I suspect that above luminous wishes,

Has kept a cruel hand, the earth's primal hunter
—this Fear.

—Nirendranath Chakravarti,
"Maulik Nishad"

The Rise and Fall of Subaltern Studies

To affirm that there are pasts and futures beyond state and capital, a collective of Indian scholars initiated the Subaltern Studies program, with the first edited volumes and monographs appearing in the 1980s. Writing in the aftermath of the decolonization of Asia and Africa, these works celebrated the resistance of Indian peasants and other laboring groups against the British Empire. Agrarian Indian militancy, embodied in fierce and continuous rebellions from the late eighteenth to the mid-twentieth century, had been the single biggest factor responsible for the collapse of the Raj. It seemed plausible to argue that the juggernaut of colonial capital—embodied by the British as well as by their elite Indian collaborators, the landed magnates, merchants, and moneylenders—had ceased its inexorable march before the iron wall of peasant community. The violent rise of Naxalite agrarian radicalism in the late 1960s and 1970s—as well as the less dramatic, but in the long run more effective ascendancy of regional middle- and lower-caste peasants in Indian politics—only served to underline that Indian political futures were forged in the communitarian countryside.

Hence Ranajit Guha, inspired in part by Antonio Gramsci, argued with conviction in the 1982 manifesto that opened the Subaltern Studies book series that subaltern life, politics, and consciousness had remained largely independent while confronting British and Indian elites. The modern state and ruling classes had failed to achieve hegemony over the minds of the subalterns: "the politics of the people" remained "an autonomous domain." In *Elementary Aspects of Peasant Insurgency in Colonial India* (1983), Guha insisted that future revolutions would build on the foundations of these subaltern rebellions. These could not be cast aside to the archaism of the "pre-political"—a term that Eric Hobsbawm had used to designate similar actors and rebellions in European history.

In *The Nation and Its Fragments* (1993), Partha Chatterjee, another leading member of the Subaltern Studies Collective, counterposed subaltern community against elite capital. According to Chatterjee, this suppressed terrain of community needed to be recovered. Community was the mode for subaltern solidarity and empowerment against the elites who were organized through bourgeois civil society and state. The subtext was clear: community was not just the anterior of capital and state but the future beyond them.

But decolonization, of course, did not eradicate the state form or capital: it only nationalized them and enabled them to proliferate. Nonwhite political classes, to defend themselves against a white-dominated global order, resorted everywhere in Asia and Africa to nation-state sovereignty. Postcolonial nation-states—India is paradigmatic—frequently promoted indigenous capitalists while placing some curbs on big property. Similar contradictions were visible in (self-declared) communist states, like the Soviet Union and China. They might have placed even more radical checks on private property, but they did little to annihilate the state form or, indeed, the logic of commodification of beings.

Marx certainly admitted in *Capital* that "private ownership of the globe by single individuals will appear quite as absurd as private ownership of one man by another. Even a whole society, a nation, or even all simultaneously existing societies taken together, are not the owners of the globe. They are only its possessors, its usufructuaries, and, like *boni patres familias*, they must hand it down to succeeding generations in an improved condition." Nevertheless, he also firmly believed in the benefits of capitalist technology. The Marxian dialectic would socialize, not annihilate, capitalist modernism. In any case, communist states showed little regard in practice to dismantling what we have called the possessive will. Authoritarian sovereignty and state capitalism interacted to make communist states some of the worst perpetrators in extracting the labor of human and nonhuman beings, in depleting and degrading the earth, to create material value.

Postcolonial (and) communist polities believed in modernity, economic growth, and progress—and expropriated agrarian lands, displaced indigenous populations, built big dams, and erected factories that polluted land, air, and water—with as much fervor as Western states. The more powerful among them—the Soviet Union, China, India, and others—were also imperious sovereigns who often annexed and ruled territories against the democratic will of local populations. If the Western bloc was culpable for Palestine and Vietnam, these states had their guilt in Hungary, Tibet, Sikkim, and the Naga Hills. In expropriating the expropriators—the imperial (and) propertied classes—the logic of the expropriators was itself preserved: the state form and the commodity form were both redistributed, rather than overthrown. Indian Naxalites dismissed the Soviet bloc as "social imperialists." Ultimately, the state-capital nexus was preserved everywhere. Commodification of beings carried on relentlessly during the Cold War: vanguarded through the agency of either state-protected big industrial capitalists or the authoritarian-bureaucratic states themselves, or through a mixed economy of state-capitalist condominium.

The 1980s and early 1990s, when the Subaltern Studies Collective was at its creative peak, were also the years when the postwar social-welfare state began to unravel, in the postcolony as in the Western metropole. Friedrich Hayek and Milton Friedman were the intellectual progenitors of this era. For neoliberalism, capital itself was sovereign— though this was often mystified, as Niklas Olsen reminds us, through the argument that the consumer was the sovereign, directing processes of production and exchange through their demands. The consumer-sovereign displaced the voter as the bearer of the democratic mandate in this mythology. Purchasing in the marketplace was theorized as equivalent to casting a ballot in an election. At base, capital itself was master. Capitalist production and exchange, embodied in variegated capitalists and consumers, ordered the world, putting to work and extracting value from beings. The Midas touch of capital turned all beings into commodities, exchangeable with money—the general equivalent subsumed all particularity of being.

Neoliberal thinkers sacralized the lordship of capital. They saw in the capitalist economy the working of a cosmic Ordo, a transhistorical rule of eternal law. Scholars today label this kind of discourse as economic theology. Giorgio Agamben, who coined the term, emphasizes how modern capitalism draws on centuries-old models of subjecting humans to celestial and earthly government. Hayek's support for the military dictatorship of Augusto Pinochet in Chile exposes the political implications of this attitude. Neoliberals recognized that the fear of the lord was necessary to force beings to work for capital. Political freedom could be dispensed with to enable the freedom of the market.

Subaltern Studies had emerged with a certain triumphalist faith: that the subaltern could historically resist state and capital. The advent of neoliberal globalization put its house in disarray. The alleged "decline of the subaltern" in Subaltern Studies—described by Sumit Sarkar—needs to be plotted onto this tectonic shift in political economy. A certain diversity in cultural life worlds could still be affirmed with conviction. After all, globalization had not really translated everywhere and equally into Westernization. It was more difficult for academics to retain faith that subaltern communitarian difference could become the launching pad for a more fundamental rearrangement of social relations between beings. Subaltern Studies was gradually subsumed into cultural studies.

In Partha Chatterjee's later works, the subaltern was no more an Other of the state but rather participated in postcolonial governance through the mediation of political society. Dipesh Chakrabarty had posited in *Provincializing Europe* (2000) two histories of capital. History 2, that of the subaltern worker, with his community life and belief in gods, spirits, and divine tools, could not be entirely subsumed within History 1, that of capitalism. By contrast, Chakrabarty's student Andrew Sartori argued in *Liberalism in Empire* (2014) that Indian peasants derived their property-based sense of freedom from being producers and sellers of commodities in a capitalist economy. They were insiders to capital, not revolutionary subalterns outside it. Sartori confesses that personally, he has "no qualms about embracing liberal norms when the alternative proffered is a romantic projection of precolonial or decolonial otherness." Ultimately, he dismisses the "availability of subalternity as an external standpoint for the critique of capitalism and colonialism."

In a similar spirit, Vivek Chibber, in *Postcolonial Theory and the Specter of Capital* (2013), suggests that the way Subaltern Studies theorized about fundamental divergences between the West and the non-West ended up "promoting" "colonialist and Orientalist presentations of the East." Like Sartori, Chibber stresses similarity rather than difference in the ways the logic of capital unfolds across the world; hence the global validity of Western ideas. "Instead of being entirely different forms of society, the West and the non-West would, according to this perspective, turn out to be variants of the same species. Further, if they are indeed variations of the same basic form, the theories generated by the European experience would not have to be overhauled or jettisoned, but simply modified." Chibber grounds his historical arguments in "some universal facts about human psychology."

The Failures of Global History
and of Anthropology

Subaltern Studies had been born from a felicitous collaboration between historians and anthropologists. However, in the early twenty-first century, historians of modernity have generally moved on to describing a world ironed out by capitalist commodity production and exchange. They have become suspicious of grand philosophical claims about non-Western alterity and are quick to dismiss these as expressions of nativism. Global history has become the vanguard of the discipline, with keywords being "circulation," "mobility," and "exchange." Global historians increasingly trace connections—movements of commodities, capital, people, germs, and ideas—between different corners of the world. Yet they generally descriptively reproduce the status quo instead of offering pathways out of it.

Global history is the academic reflection of a world bound by neoliberal capitalism—it embodies the rule of capital, even when recalcitrant against its sway. Neoliberal academia is replete with scholars today who claim radicalness but refuse alternatives to state and capital—who profess incredulity and anger about the conviction that there can be other ways of being. They see decolonization as a phenomenon of the past, not as an ongoing struggle.

Simultaneously, the glass of anthropological knowledge has become darkened by despondency, dystopian, and extinction theories. The earth is exhausted, and ontologies are dying. Many anthropological monographs read as funeral rites for communities. Alternatively, anthropologists offer hyper-micro studies of specific communities and their life worlds that still resist modern state and capital. But they leave unclear whether these life worlds can offer any pathways out of the state-capital nexus that rules the planet.

In fetishizing the microscopic, anthropology has turned inward and abrogated its public responsibility. Once, anthropologists wanted to enhance our understanding of and empathy toward other ways of living—to borrow Ruth Benedict's words, to enable "a world made safe for differences." Today, they cannot see beyond what Joel Robbins calls the "suffering subject."

In the *Divine Comedy*, Dante, guided by the Roman poet Virgil, travels the circles of Inferno, where anger and suffering "always whirl in dark timeless (*sanza tempo*) air." Anthropologists similarly follow the suffering subject, recounting near-identical stories. The annihilation of forests implies the annihilation of ancestors and spirits; the melting of glaciers translates into deities abandoning their mountain abodes; despoliation, dispossession, and ruin are everywhere. The abstract time of capital is truly a time without time, *sanza tempo*, denuded of Being. In hell, everything repeats itself, though all things seem in tumult.

Anthropologists dissect every term—"indigeneity," "conservation," "human rights," "sustainable development"—to show how they are all riddled with flaws. They bemoan how communities are becoming proto-states and paracorporations in the very process of wrestling with state and capital. John and Jean Comaroff label this *Ethnicity, Inc.*—ethnic groups run as businesses and sell themselves as brands while claiming shares in sovereignty. Ultimately, there remains little difference between historians who describe the world and do not know how to transform it and anthropologists who cannot think except in lament.

But what Sherry Ortner calls "dark anthropology"—the current mood of anthropology, witnessing Inferno—cannot be the destination of the discipline. Anthropology must also point to Paradiso. In learning from human communities who are resisting state and capital across the world today, we shall expand our circles of empathy. Nonhuman beings shall inspire us to transhuman ourselves. We must stream into other beings, share intelligence, be-in-common.

History and anthropology have stood accused at various moments of being the priests of imperialism, dividing peoples into categories of superior (those with state and civilization, proper subjects of history) and inferior (those without, and hence subjects of anthropology). The present conjuncture invites both disciplines to redeem themselves from this condominium. This requires the dethroning of Anthropos as earth-monarch, solitary species-sovereign.

To Arms: A New Academia for a Renewed War

We need to act now in full recognition of the livingness, awakeness, agency, and entanglements of beings—nonhuman and human—who constitute the cosmos. To escape Inferno, we need pan-being sustainable intelligence. These alternative lifeways shall be grounded in care and curiosity toward a world in which humans are only one among many beings—and certainly not the only ones who speak, represent, enact, and own history. New forms of ethics and justice must be grounded in the reality that humans and other-than-humans are so enmeshed that violence and dispossession enacted upon the one inevitably injure the other. Each act of ours must proclaim that justice, to be just, must be more than human. The world can only flourish as multibeing constitution.

This is the labor of this century, for which history and anthropology must inhabit each other. Intellectual history allows anthropology to see how its recent turns regarding the nonhuman and the ontological are the latest renditions of millennia-old forms of thought. History tells anthropology that our epoch is best characterized as "The Great Exile," and that the foregrounding of the relational mode between humans and nonhumans in a recent and promising (albeit still marginal) scholarship is as much a project of unlearning the impressions of capitalist modernity as a new realization.

Now is an auspicious time for such augury. For the neoliberal order—seemingly in its moment of greatest triumph—confronts the most diverse legions of enemies it has hitherto encountered. The forces are unequal, but the voices denounce. Black and Dalit movements speak against the diverse ways capital deploys age-old hierarchies of race and caste to ensure a steady and hereditary supply of laboring bodies. Trans actors organize rebellious modes of kinship to achieve mutual aid, material and emotional care.

Feminist and queer activists challenge the primitive accumulation, primal capture of the womb—the production and reproduction of household labor on whose basis alone male work and male sovereignty can subsist. Marxist-feminist scholar-activist Tithi Bhattacharya distinguishes between life-making and thing-making. She asks for social relations to be comprehensively reorganized, so that life-making—far more entrusted to women than to men—takes precedence over capitalist commodity and profit creation.

Social reproduction theorists condemn the undervaluation of women's labor as wives, as nurses, as teachers in primary schools, as domestic servants. The edifice of the wage form subsists on women's unwaged care work. Françoise Vergès draws inspiration from the strike by Black and Brown cleaning women at the Gare du Nord train station in Paris in 2018. She champions a decolonial feminism that would acknowledge how women, especially underpaid or unpaid nonwhite women, clean up the toxic waste and ruination left by capitalism. Feminist struggles must dismantle the racial Capitalocene.

Veronica Gago theorizes about a dynamic power that would arise from the International Women's Strikes of 2017-18, against the ongoing femicide across the world. In Argentina and across South America, such action has galvanized novel forms of assembly, uniting female, queer, Indigenous, and environmentalist demands against white male regimes of value extraction. Gago celebrates these strikes as apparatuses of "collective intelligence."

From the Niyamgiri hills of India to Dakota in the United States, Indigenous populations raise their fists against neocolonial corporations and technologies of commodifying and devastating human and nonhuman communities. From Parliament Square in London to rail tracks in Oregon, the Extinction Rebellion fosters decentralized grassroots struggles of civil disobedience to impel public action against the extinction of species and ongoing climate catastrophe. The year 2019 saw the largest wave of climate strikes in human history, involving more than six million people across 150 countries.

The house of academics may be divided, but the worlds of protest against capital—and its guardian, the state—continue to move and converge. It is imperative in this moment to unite the forces of history and anthropology to aid the already existing struggles against capital and state. Historians and anthropologists sit on reservoirs of traditional knowledge, but they do not always know, or even believe, that this knowledge can nourish contemporary revolution. Our manifesto calls them to arms.

Enough of Welfare-State Capitalism

The economist Thomas Piketty argues that the present neoliberal order represents a peak in class inequality across the world. In *Capital and Ideology*, Piketty observes that the share of the highest-earning 10 percent of the population in the income distribution across India, the United States, Russia, China, and Europe "stood at around 25–35 percent in 1980 but by 2018 had risen to between 35 and 55 percent." This "increase in inequality has come at the expense of the bottom 50 percent of the distribution, whose share of total income stood at about 20–25 percent in 1980 in all five regions but had fallen to 15–20 percent in 2018 (and, indeed, as low as 10 percent in the United States)." Meanwhile, "the top decile claimed 54 percent of total income in sub-Saharan Africa (and as much as 65 percent in South Africa), 56 percent in Brazil, and 64 percent in the Middle East."

Piketty suggests that to overcome this catastrophic class inequality, the state should again pursue social-welfarist programs of wealth redistribution. Every young adult should be given an initial capital fund, financed by rigorous progressive taxation. Piketty wants to make ownership "temporary" and "social" and ensure wider circulation of wealth, but not to abolish the logic of ownership and material wealth as such. Hence his remedies for the climate crisis—mainly, progressive taxation on carbon emissions—remain inadequate.

Piketty wants to preserve the state form as well as the logic of capitalist production. States should cooperate with each other in ensuring high taxation of transnational corporations rather than compete against each other to lure businesses with the seduction of low taxes. They should use the resultant surplus to improve education, health care, and other social provisions for the multitudes. Piketty hopes that young adults will use their capital fund to buy houses and start businesses. This is similar to the Nobel Laureates Abhijit Banerjee and Esther Duflo's recommendation, in *Poor Economics*, "to recognize the nascent capitalist inside every poor man and woman," in order to address poverty.

In contrast to these economists, we argue that there needs to be an assault against the logic of capitalist production—based on the commodification of human and nonhuman beings, of the earth—itself. There needs to be an assault on centralized state sovereignty, which everywhere protects capitalist production.

The failure of the United Nations Framework Convention on Climate Change 1992—extended by the Kyoto Protocol 1997; Copenhagen Accord 2009; Paris Agreement 2015—to tackle the climate crisis hints at the root problem. States are guardians of capital; a wolf pack cannot protect the sheep. Among states, high-income countries, led by the United States, dominate the international economic order through institutions like the World Bank and the International Monetary Fund. Interstate cooperation is too fragile, as President Donald Trump's withdrawal of the United States from the Paris Agreement laid bare. Frequently, only lowest-common-denominator action wins, as the G7 agreement on a minimum global corporation tax in 2021 has recently demonstrated. Even Piketty sees here "the formalisation of a real licence to defraud for the most powerful players."

Mere redistribution of resources by a centralized state is not enough, as the tragic histories of decolonization and Cold War communism have shown. We need a deeper transnational politics than one driven by interstate agreements: one based not on reinforcing but on dismantling the power of states. We need a new internationalism rooted in nonstate communities and their transnational solidarities. Anthropologists should be in arms to offer policy recommendations here, based on their deep knowledge of Indigenous communities and landscapes, where beings are often still beings—where the welfare of nonhuman beings carries weight in public deliberation.

Enough of Monstrous Abstractions!

How did the degeneration of beings into things take place? How did Being transform into abstractions: commodity, capital, and labor? Taking a cue from Marx, Alfred Sohn-Rethel suggests that commodity exchange involved dissimilar entities being rendered equivalent, with this equivalence embodied in money, the universal equivalent. Thus from commodity exchange arose a society mediated and governed by real abstraction.

We propose a more originary transformation. In the beginning was Being-beings. As some human beings put other beings, human and nonhuman, to work, there occurred a primal degeneration of being as well as a disease of language. The first step was the production of mythic image arguments—for the Khasi, the vampire-serpent sucks human blood in order to generate wealth; for the Bakweri, the master turns humans into zombies to put them to work. In the first flush of encounter with capital, humans everywhere see the process of commodification as monster making.

In the second step, these images coagulated into abstract theoretical arguments, as in Marx, though still bearing the trace of the original monstrosity. "Capital is dead labour, that, vampire-like, only lives by sucking living labour, and lives the more, the more labour it sucks." And again, in *Capital*: "For 'protection' against 'the serpent of their agonies,' the labourers must put their heads together."

However, for Marx's argument to arise—for abstract categories like labor and capital to form—there needed already to be a decay of being. These real abstractions arise from the setting of the sun of being.

Being shines through trees, in the eyes of the raven, in the waters of the burn when the sun dances on it: it is eroded as the streams are polluted, trees felled, and birds and beasts exiled to extinction. Dead labor arises not only on the corpse of being but as a second step after various humans have already conceptualized the degeneration of being, the erosion of life, as sucking blood, making zombies, and other perversions. Beings degenerate into snakes, into the undead, before coagulating into abstractions: capital (the erstwhile blood-sucking snake and vampire), labor (the zombie). Nature, as real abstraction, hunting ground of capital, also arises from the cremation of beings.

As a third and final step, Marx declares in *Capital* that he will deal with individuals only as the personification of economic categories, as bearers of certain class relations and interests. The capitalist, for him, is only capital personified. Beings were the first denizens of the universe, from whose degeneration arose real abstractions, categories of political economy. Now the real abstractions, capital and labor, become primary while real beings become just their aftereffects. Through this complete reversal, the category of interest—prime mover of capitalist production, exchange, and consumption—is constituted. Self-interest becomes the great social mediation in capitalism. This is the ultimate perversion and inversion of being and language.

Where Marx Went Wrong

Hence even someone so keen-sighted as Marx swerves off in the wrong direction when he thinks that revolution can come at the hands of the proletariat, the universal class, the expropriated who will expropriate the expropriators. How can this happen when the universal class—itself, of course, a conceptual borrowing from Hegel's definition of the state bureaucracy—is a mere coagulation of degenerated beings? Revolution cannot come from these coagulations produced by state and capital, when beings have been steamrolled into a universal abstraction. The logic of capital does not pave the way for its own dissolution. There is no iron law of necessity in history. Conditions of oppression—being proletariat—cannot magically turn into conditions of liberation through some mythic overcoming.

Revolution will never arise from the logic of capital. Whenever the expropriated expropriate the expropriators, the logic of exploitation is preserved. The histories of decolonization and Cold War communism testify to this. To bring revolution, we have to return to what is logically anterior to these real abstractions, what is logically other to capital—that is, to beings themselves in all the diversity of their beingness. It is in exposing and connecting that diversity that the secret hope of revolution lies. Marx was right in emphasizing the poetry of revolution, and utterly wrong in thinking that the poetry of the future cannot draw upon the past. But before we demonstrate this, let us chart the steps through which language decayed even as Being was eclipsed.

> I picked up a clumsy log
> And threw it at the water-trough with a clatter.
> […]
> And immediately I regretted it.
> I thought how paltry, how vulgar, what a mean
>   act!
> I despised myself and the voices of my accursed
>   human education.
>
> And I thought of the albatross,
> And I wished he would come back, my snake.
> […]
> And so, I missed my chance with one of the
>   lords
> Of life.
> And I have something to expiate:
> A pettiness.
>   —D. H. Lawrence, "Snake"

The Degeneration of Speech

Many, perhaps most, historical societies have discussed, in one or another form, communication between humans and nonhumans. In India, from the *Jataka* and *Panchatantra* stories of early historical times, to the *Chandimangal* and *Manasamangal* traditions of the early modern period, to beliefs about Bonbibi "Lady of the Forest" and the tiger god Dakshin Ray today, tigers, lions, elephants, snakes, birds, monkeys, trees have all been invested with the ability to speak to humans, to admonish them. In the Indian imagination, the political has never been a human monopoly. Rather, nonhumans have always been considered, even to this day, as political agents with whom humans have to share in decision making. The *Brihadaranyaka Upanishad* records how the voice of the thunder enjoins us to constantly practice self-control, giving, and compassion—a chant immortalized for the twentieth century by the grand finale of T. S. Eliot's *The Waste Land*. In Greece, the sacred grove of Dodona was an oracle, and dryads, naiads, and nereids made trees, streams, and the sea speak with unerring regularity.

The first fall occurred when some human societies expelled nonhuman beings from their speech—and by extension, political—community. Domesticating the nonhuman would culminate in their muting: as a halfway to this, the Roman Varro designated animals as semivocal instruments. From early medieval Europe to modern northeastern India, Christian missionaries cut down sacred groves, silencing trees. Hegel derided ancient Egypt for zoolatry, for revering divine-human-animal hybrids, exemplified by the Sphinx and by Anubis. He felt that European civilization had rightly replaced the worship of the animal with veneration of nature as abstraction. Modern man became sovereign by cutting off the nonhuman who had earlier shared his vocal and political community, the space of his liturgy.

> Never, oh never is the arrow meet
> For piercing the tender body of a deer,
> As the fire is not
> For burning flowers.
>
> —Kalidasa, *Shakuntala*,
> tr. Rabindranath Tagore

In the second fall—we say this in terms of logic, rather than strict history; in history, the various falls discussed here intersected—humans divided each other, expelling each other from their communities. The ancient Greek *barbaros* and the Sanskritic *barbara* alike designate the foreigner who speaks unintelligibly, who has been estranged on the basis of his speech. In the Bible, God divides human beings into speakers of many languages so that they will not reach heaven and presumably challenge his sovereignty.

In the third fall within these speech communities, the women were silenced. In the First Epistle to the Corinthians in the New Testament, women are notoriously asked to be silent in the church, the assembly par excellence for Christians. Among the Nagas of northeastern India, there is a still resilient notion of community thinking and community voice, but women are marginalized in the public assemblies.

In the fourth fall, community speech—at least, whatever remained of collective speech after the expulsion of the nonhuman, the foreigner, and the woman—too decayed. Initially, some privileged groups, like the Brahmins in India and the jurists in Rome, claimed to be authoritative interpreters of community law, even as they usurped the will of the community. Finally, there was a climactic individualization of speech. The sovereign master said, "I will," and the state was born. For Justinianic Roman law, revived in late medieval Europe, what pleased the prince had the force of law. In Hegel's Germany and in John Austin's England, the will and command of the sovereign—not the collective voice of community, as among the Nagas—made law.

The individual property owner similarly said, "This is mine," and enclosed what belonged to the commons: the agricultural land, the pastures, the village ponds. This speech polluted the common air and streams. Individualized speech was inscribed into writing: bureaucracy, account keeping, debt records arose on the debris of collective living speech. The collectives have now become resources—labor and inert nature, made calculable for exploitation. Gayatri

Chakravorty Spivak's momentous question—Can the sub-altern speak?—could only arise in this era, when speech has become individualized, when being atrophies. The epoch when speech and being were alike collective, born from the flows of life between beings, mirror on mirror each being for another—rather than from the craig of the sovereign, solitary perch of the private proprietor—has truly passed away. Only now, therefore, does the question acquire any salience. How could it have been asked in any previous era?

The Poetry of Revolution

The account we gave above is grounded in reliable history and ethnography but is not itself, in the strict sense, historical or ethnographic. It abstracts many historical transformations into an encompassing narrative. The poetry of the future, to return to Marx's expression in *The Eighteenth Brumaire of Louis Bonaparte*, has the duty to overcome the great exclusion sketched above. Yet how shall this be done? In the Sanskritic tradition, the first verse—beginning *ma nishada*, You may not, o hunter!—arose when Valmiki saw a hunter kill a male crane making love to his partner. The very first poem in the world is thus an interdiction against violence. But what poetics is adequate now against the sixth extinction—against the relentless necropolitics that transforms living beings into meat, fat, fertilizers, things?

In *The Great Derangement*, Amitav Ghosh laments the absolute failure of modern literature in addressing the climate crisis. This is unsurprising, given modern literature's role in upholding state and capital. Gauri Viswanathan shows how English literature was disseminated to the colonies as "masks of conquest," to extract loyalty from subject peoples. Lisa Lowe reveals how imperial extraction of labor and resources shaped English prose. During the Cold War, American cultural policies—organized through networks like the CIA-funded Congress for Cultural Freedom—encouraged a hyperindividualized, privatized, and psychologized realm of self and domesticity in literature. Broader social struggles were seen as unworthy of art. The novel became ever more a bourgeois form.

How can we imagine a future poetics beyond state and capital? In her recent books *Ganatantrer Rahasya* and *Yukti o Kalpanashakti*, Gayatri Chakravorty Spivak suggests that democracy cannot be reduced to the arithmetic of votes, to the machinery of the state (*rashtrer kal*). Similarly, anticapitalist revolution cannot derive its content from the value form of capital. Instead, democracy—and indeed, revolution—needs poiesis, poetry, *kavya*, *kavita*, which connect human beings. *Kalpanashakti*—the power of imagination—empowers the other (*apara*) to haunt us; it is *aparashakti*. It trains us to transcend greed and self-interest. The mystery of democracy, of revolution, lies in this haunting that connects beings.

In the ancient Vedic canon, poetry involved creating *bandhus*, connections, between beings. In modern

Bengali, the word for literature, *sahitya*, stems from *sahit*, to be together with. In Sanskrit and in Bengali, *sahitya* originally meant association, society—and thence took on the meaning of literary composition. Literature enables overcoming the alienation of Being into commodities: poetry is the restoration of togetherness. Literature is society.

However, literature needs to be allied to existing emancipatory struggles by the oppressed. The case of Martin Heidegger—whose alienation from modernity led him into dangerous cohabitation with Nazism—shows the dangers of asking for a revitalization of poetics, of Being, when disjointed from subaltern revolution. The revitalization then runs the risk of sliding into a romance of reaction, if not outright fascism. By contrast, we ask: What poetry can there be that does not denounce capital? That does not curse the state?

The poetic form in which nonhumans speak to and instruct humans is as old as time. It acquires urgency in an era when bourgeois democracies thump their chests in reflecting the will of the people—however misleading in fact this self-congratulation—but feel no burning shame in excluding nonhumans from constitutional community. "We the people" is a badge of dishonor if it cannot reflect on the original sin of exiling the nonhuman from the political.

Enough of "Postmodern" Suspicion of Being!

How shall we reverse this great exile that has relegated nonhuman beings to unbeing? To even raise this question implies squarely facing something that has become a cultural embarrassment in recent decades: the question of Being. Jean-François Lyotard famously spoke in 1979 about "the postmodern condition" as involving an "incredulity toward metanarratives." He rightly denounced the way that Heidegger had related the affirmation of Being to the legitimation of Nazism and correctly linked the decline of these metanarratives to the individualized consumption patterns produced by advanced capitalism. But he failed to transform the question of Being into a struggle for overcoming capital.

Exhausted by the Second World War, confronted with the barbarity of the Holocaust, threatened by Soviet communism, challenged by anticolonial politics—all of which put in doubt shibboleths of Western civilization and progress—intellectuals in the Western world lost confidence in the grand beliefs that had undergirded Europe for the previous three millennia. Any firm belief appeared as a royal road to the concentration camp and the gulag. In Lyotard's words: "The nineteenth and twentieth centuries have given us as much terror as we can take. We have paid a high enough price for the nostalgia of the whole and the one [...]. Let us wage a war on totality."

Jacques Derrida's *Of Grammatology* (1967) is perhaps the greatest expression of this rejection. Derrida was skeptical and condescending toward all those concepts—*ousia, parousia, logos, eidos*, and so on—that had grounded European philosophical and political certitude from ancient Greece through the era of Christianity to the Enlightenment and beyond. Yet in putting Being, *ousia*, to question, in dismantling any possibility of an originary innocence and purity that could be restored, Derrida struck at the roots of any redemptive politics that would ground itself in such faith. He doubted that the Indigenous Nambikwara people of Brazil might hold clues for a more equal and just world that the West could learn from. This appeared as a fantasy of originary Being and natural goodness that required deconstruction.

Today, when Indigenous peoples are at the forefront of decolonial and environmentalist battles against Western-led capital, such a reading appears naïve, if not tinged with colonial arrogance. The peoples of Amazonia need the world to affirm, not question, their goodness. Derrida's presentation of writing against the authenticity claims of the spoken word, *logos*, as present in Nambikwara assemblies and elsewhere, appears equally pointless today. The relevant question now is not whether writing has superseded speech but how capital commodifies speech as well as writing, from genes to the internet to every media space.

Similarly, reading *A Thousand Plateaus* (1980) by Gilles Deleuze and Félix Guattari today, one is astonished at the glib championing of the rhizomatic society against the rooted one. The rhizome "carries enough force to shake and uproot the verb 'to be.'" One understands *historically* why such arguments became attractive in post-Holocaust, postwar Europe. It is less easy today to *politically* sympathize with arguments that celebrate the settler colonialism of the American frontier as a model of the rhizomatic society. When Native Americans, Maori peoples, Indigenous Hawaiians, Adivasi and Dalit communities, Kashmiris, Palestinians, Kurds, Uyghurs, Nagas, and Tibetans all derive their strength from their rooted communities—when they use those roots to combat White or Brown settler colonials who invade and desecrate their lands—what political purpose is served by the animus against the root? The celebration of the rhizome is an apologia for the rootlessness of capital. The uprooting of Being, of human and nonhuman beings, only eases expropriation and reification. It would be the ultimate cunning of capitalist reason if future generations see the primitive accumulation of neoliberal capital as the most enduring practical legacy of postmodernism—sovereign capital meditating invincible on the cremation ground of every other dismantled value, deconstructed solidarity.

The Road Back to Being

Asato ma sadgamaya
From Unbeing lead me to Being.
Tamaso ma jyotirgamaya
From darkness lead me to light.

Our thirst for possession, craving for profit, congeals as capital. In a reversal, capital makes nonhuman beings appear as things; human beings as congealed labor; corporations—states and companies—as persons. Property claims inalienable rights; rights are denied to sentient beings. Commodity veils Being. Our desire to protect our possessions from others congeals as state. The state guarantees *mamedam*, this is mine. Neighbors manifest as enemies. Politics becomes war.

Mrityormamritam gamaya
From death lead me to immortality.

Advocates of degrowth clamor that we have to limit our desires and cease to be hostages to GDP metrics. Giorgos Kallis in his book *Degrowth* and Jason Hickel in *Less Is More* show how our thirst for endless consumption fuels economic growth and precipitates rising carbon emissions, global warming, mineral extraction, pollution, and extinction of nonhuman species. The model of "green growth" is a mirage. Population control offers no remedy as long as consumption, particularly by the rich, does not lessen. Hickel observes: "The richest 10% of the world's population are responsible for almost half the world's total lifestyle carbon emissions. In other words, the global climate crisis is being driven largely by the global rich. [...] The richest 1% emit thirty times more than the poorest 50% of the human population."

Degrowth advocates are unanimous in prescribing the scaling down of extraction, production, and exchange. They offer varied pathways: giving land back to peasants and other Indigenous communities; restricting mining, the fossil fuel industry, and the industrial meat sector; limiting advertising; reducing working hours; creating ceilings on the size of houses and sports stadiums; banning a range of commodities, from single-use plastics and coffee cups to SUVs; creating a commons of resources, from cars to garden tools, shifting from individual purchase to a community of goods. Ultimately, it boils down to radically downscaling consumption—channeling hours from growth-oriented work to nonprofit social relations. The Buddha was right after all. Thirst must be restrained: *tanha* leads to *dukkha*.

"In the midst of water, I am driven by thirst." To escape the Necrocene, beings must be recognized as life. Freedom lies in the interdependence of Being.

Ritam vadishyami, satyam vadishyami

Capital enchants us to see subjects as objects, objects as subjects. The central dialectic of Subaltern Studies 2.0 should be to reverse the reversal—retransforming, reawakening objects into subjects, stripping subjecthood from capital. The light of Being fades but never completely recedes from the horizon, like the sun on a cloudless mid-summer night.

Human and Other-than-human Beings, you alone are visible Being, you alone are Real. We announce you as Right, we proclaim you as True.

Dismantle State, Overthrow Capital!

Who shall offer the organizational apparatus for this change? Like Piketty, Kallis and Hickel mainly rely on the effectiveness of middle-class civil-society agitation and the goodwill of states to bring about policies to ensure social and environmental justice. Their critique of capital is not matched by any desire to overthrow the state. Kallis admits in *Degrowth*: "It took two world wars and millions of deaths for the nation state system to stabilize—we should think twice before advocating its collapse." (This statement is misleading; it ignores the role of decolonization, which forms an arc from the late eighteenth century—Haiti and Latin America—to the late twentieth, globalizing the nation-state system beyond Europe.)

In fact, the overthrow of capital is impossible without the overthrow of the state. If states persist, then—as the examples of the Soviet Union and decolonization in Asia and Africa have shown—capitalism always creeps back in, first as state capital, then as private capital. As long as states remain, they will compete with each other militarily, continually spurring GDP-led growth in the process. Production is war by other means.

Hickel is prepared to learn from Indigenous communities about better ways of managing human-nonhuman relations; after all, scientists "estimate that 80% of the planet's biodiversity is to be found on territories stewarded by Indigenous peoples." But he emphasizes ameliorating existing public policies and institutions, rather than unraveling them to let non-Western community forms take over. He largely treats the Indigenous communities as sources of alternative knowledge rather than alternative *political* formations that can take control of the world.

Meanwhile, Andreas Malm advises us to blow up pipelines, bomb petrol stations, damage SUVs, and perform other acts of material damage to the infrastructure of capital, courting prison. But this advice remains too dependent again on middle-class conscience. There is no sense of the larger communities, particularly in the non-Western world, where such activism can find roots. Karen Bell admits how these "groups, such as Extinction Rebellion [...] are not strongly rooted in working-class organisations and communities."

Where shall we find these mass organizations and communities? In *Assembly*, Michael Hardt and Antonio Negri ask us "to invent new, nonsovereign institutions" and nonproperty forms. They find precapitalist communities homogeneously "disgusting," too infected with hierarchy and inequality to be politically useful. Their attitude is comparable to Hobsbawm's condescension toward precapitalist struggles as pre-political, which Ranajit Guha denounced decades ago. *Assembly* refuses to engage with centuries-old Dalit-Bahujan, Adivasi, and other Indigenous forms of participatory democracy, wealth sharing, and social commoning *already* prevalent across the world.

Hardt and Negri assert, against all historical and ethnographic evidence, "that people are not innately capable of collective self-rule and that democracy is not and cannot be spontaneous." We say instead: We have always been democrats! Democracy has never been all-inclusive. But from ancient Indian *gana* polities and Greek city-states to acephalous polities in Aboriginal Australia and the Indigenous Americas, self-ruling collectives are natural and primordial to humanity. Democracy is an ancient way of life—not a modern invention. In fact, when ruling classes have claimed to invent democracy by building institutions of governance—constitutions, bureaucracies, and all the rest—they have, more often than not, created bourgeois states rather than living, thriving, democracies. Postcolonial Asia and Africa offer many examples of this degeneration.

For Permanent Revolution, Permanent Community!

Let us be clear. To resist state and capital, we need solidarities. For solidarities to be viable, some enduring sense of community is needed. For permanent revolution, we need permanent community. Too much has been said in criticism of community, too little about its importance for life. The baby has been thrown out with the bathwater. Yet humans and nonhumans have lived in interdependent communities for millennia. Beings depend on each other like speech and meaning. Community is what most of the world will need as climate change takes its toll, Bangladesh is flooded, island nations sink, Africa becomes too hot to live in. We shall live. We shall win. In the short run, nothing changes; in the long run, everything changes; we just have to outlive and outsmart capitalism.

But to appreciate community, a fundamental change in cognition is necessary among middle-class thinkers. Mark Fisher famously defined the sensibility of Capitalist Realism: capitalism portraying itself as the only reality, the end of which becomes impossible to imagine. In fact, capital treats us with a tough love. It debilitates us only to sell us balms for our exhaustion, so that we cling to it the more it holds us hostage: after a hard day of working for a company, Netflix and chill rather than community work.

By contrast, community enjoins us, often to irrational excess, to remain always strong and fortified. To overthrow capitalism, to dismantle the state, many will have to confront prison and death, as was the case during the great anticolonial struggles of Asia and Africa. People can die as soldiers and policemen, or they can die for their communities. "Greater love hath no man than this, that a man lay down his life for his friends."

Enough of Atomized Individualism!

After many decades, intellectuals are once more confidently restoring the community above the atomized individual. Donna Haraway emphasizes the importance of making kin in the Age of the Chthulucene (a neologism from the Greek word for earth). Discarding the "bounded individualism" of the Anthropocene, she emphasizes multispecies symbiosis, sympoiesis, "making-with." She announces, "We are all lichens." The old-new gods of the new age are Gaia, Earth recognized as a superorganism; Potnia Theron, Lady of Animals.

Feminist and queer activists today lead the struggle in rejecting capitalist atomization. They draw strength from earlier moments such as the Combahee River Collective Statement of 1977, issued by the American Black feminist lesbian socialist organization: "Although we are feminists and Lesbians, we feel solidarity with progressive Black men and do not advocate the fractionalization that white women who are separatists demand. Our situation as Black people necessitates that we have solidarity around the fact of race, which white women of course do not need to have with white men."

Françoise Vergès rejects the individualistic girl power model as symptomatic of white-capitalist feminism, finding it unsuitable for nonwhite women's struggles. Against popular culture celebration of exceptional women, where the "struggle is rarely collective," she posits nonwhite women's deep histories. "This is what songs of struggle—Black spirituals, revolutionary songs, gospel songs, songs of slaves and colonized people—recount: the long road to freedom, a never-ending struggle, revolution as daily work."

Veronica Gago argues that "the figure of the individual as owner is inexorably masculine, an idea that is foundational to patriarchy." She celebrates a feminist politics that "is able to take root and territorialize itself in concrete struggles"—"an internationalism that finds inspiration in the autonomous struggles of Rojava and communitarian struggles in Guatemala, in the struggles of Chilean students and favela dwellers in Brazil, of campesinas in Paraguay and Afro-Colombian women." Gago observes: "Feminism makes explicit something that is not always obvious: that nobody lacks a territory." Feminist internationalism is built from "territories in struggle," involving "common invention against expropriation, collective enjoyment against privatization."

Trans activist-thinker Dean Spade similarly asks us to build postcapitalist societies through mutual aid and interdependence. The Sylvia Rivera Law Project, a New York-based law collective Spade worked with for two decades, which serves marginalized trans and gender-nonconforming people, exemplifies such an endeavor. Jules Joanne Gleeson and Nathaniel Dickson observe that trans politics demands "reassociation" and "reunification," "easing us out of the over-individuation required for us to weather harsher periods."

We do not prescribe utopia as a determinate form of political system or administration, of people or of things. Instead, we advocate a continuous process of realizing Being through the interdependence and mutual aid among beings. Similarly, we understand community in two ways: first as a process rather than an existing monolith, something that is always in advent rather than already achieved. However, in our second meaning, we take as our base communities that already exist—especially, much like Subaltern Studies 1.0, communities of the oppressed.

The Left has failed wherever it has sought to build communities from above, replacing existing communities by abstractions like the proletariat—in practice, the party usurping the place of the subaltern. The histories of the Soviet Union and of China are replete with tragedies of the party-state crushing existing subaltern communities. In India, the mainstream parliamentary Left—led by a Brahmanical intelligentsia—failed primarily because it could not work with Dalit-Bahujan and Adivasi-Indigenous communities in most parts of the subcontinent. Barring some exceptions, these communities were generally subordinated to the party organization and its high-caste leadership rather than allowed to be the vanguard of communist politics. Revolution can never be achieved in this way, by an abstraction claiming to be the "universal class"; it can only be achieved through a heterogeneous coalition of communities-in-solidarity.

Not Universal Class,
but Communities in Solidarity!

The goal of Subaltern Studies 2.0 should be to avoid the mainstream Left's past errors. This also means that we ought to study how subaltern actors themselves conceptualize community, rather than impose on them our reifying abstractions. In South Asia, subaltern actors recognize that actually existing communities are infected by internal hierarchies of class and gender, while also being oppressed by ruling classes from above. Rather than advocate a naïve communitarianism that encloses communities and reinforces these hierarchies, Dalit-Bahujan-Adivasi-Indigenous actors have frequently sought to create solidarities among subaltern communities, in order to dissolve internal and external inequalities. Out of this politics, Subaltern Studies 2.0 draws its vision of rooted interdependence. But to understand how subaltern actors themselves understand community, let us begin with the Nagas.

> We are not unaware of other people's opinion of us: they call us "primitive." Yet, with all our primitiveness, you see smiling face spontaneously beaming on

*you wherever you go. [...] What is the source of this
happy outcome? It is in the foundation of our "community" system.*

So spoke A. Z. Phizo, the Naga visionary, in 1951,
in the aftermath of India's independence, calling for the
devolution of sovereignty to the Naga "community-group
organization." The Naga bid for a stateless postcolonial
future was crushed by the military and paramilitary forces
of the Indian state. Decolonization was left incomplete—
the independent Indian state revealed its coloniality. But
the world's longest-running rebellion continues in various
forms. (The fragments interposed in italics below are also
by Phizo.)

Phizo had placed the word "community" within quo-
tation marks. Indeed, in many Naga languages there is no
term that exactly translates the English word. The extreme
decentralization traditionally prevalent among Nagas prevented the emergence of a singular concept of community
across village borders. Pluralism opposed logocentrism.
A Western political theorist might retort that the Nagas
lacked the capability of conceptual abstraction. State and
capital would lift them from the concrete to the abstract,
the particular to the general, the primitive to the civi-
lized. In contrast, we argue that the very absence of such
an abstraction reveals alternative modes of community
making that do not rely on homogenization. Here, the
community is not a mere para-state, a state in sheep's
clothing.

In sublating the Nagas into bourgeois civil society, Indian state and capital ripped Naga time into two tenses. For the first time, the past became a truly foreign country. Naga elders—like their Indigenous counterparts nearly everywhere else—now lament that life was far better in the past, when everyone was more cooperative and the air was fresh. The present is felt to be an age of decline. Electoral democracy and capitalist development are identified as signs of corruption; in a necessary dialectic, liberalism becomes heteronomy. Nevertheless, we believe that there still persists a distinctly Naga grammar of assembly and agreement making that can provide us a pathway to overcome state and capital.

> *We are strong enough to be very individualistic but*
> *we also know that man cannot live by himself alone.*
> *We had to abide by community and public opinion,*
> *and our fathers struggled hard for all these good*
> *things our nation enjoy today.*

Bourgeois individualism is fake individualism. Capital subordinates the bulk of humanity to the unloved drudgery of work, inhibits human flourishing and creativity, and only offers limited satisfaction of human desires through the consumption of commodities. The nation-state yokes humans to majoritarian identities and is the stubborn opponent of true diversity. Against the fake individualism offered by capital and state citizenship stands the Naga model, which realizes and grounds individuality through community. The community is not the antithesis of the individual but their conduit.

A Naga assembly works through a dialectic that seeks to reconcile the diversity of voices with the necessity of agreement. Hence these meetings tend to be lengthy, sometimes stretching for days. Any immediate decision through voting is abhorred, as this would create winners and losers. No decision is usually preferred over a divisive decision—the goal being to shape a collective through reciprocity and discussion, rather than through majoritarian unity. Finally, when a decision is arrived at, it often does not represent the village majority but is the viewpoint with which the fewest members vehemently disagree. In Chokri Naga, this decision is called *müthikülü*, literally, the voice of the assembly. Individuals commit to this through the solemn utterance *müthikülü Omüdozo*, "to the voice of the assembly, I agree." It is considered immoral for anyone to criticize or backpedal on an assembly agreement.

Here is a sophisticated grammar of agreement building, more refined in many ways than the brute logic of first-past-the-post poll victories or majoritarian legislation present in modern electoral democracies. When there are disputes and disagreements, they are deliberated on through *küdzükhoküyi*, agreement making. Agreements are sealed through an oath (*rüswu*), a sacred covenant sworn on the lives of the oath takers and their kindred and symbolized by the breaking of a spear, the biting of a bullet, or, more recently, a hand on the Bible.

We uphold that it is an honor to recognize the dignity of personal responsibility, and we consider as a privilege to be of service to others which our culture has given the expression we call mhosho—*to excel (*mho, *overhead;* so, *touch). Was there any Naga citizen who over fallen into trouble and left to his and her own fate? This did not happen in our memory.*

The Naga assembly silences none. However, this is not pure egalitarianism—and here lies both the assembly's strength and its weakness. The sonority of each voice is weighed according to the words-giver's previous acts of service to others. This is an ontology of social differentiation that places the collective over individuals, those regarded as more meritorious—the brave, the generous, the wise—over those seen as less so. In this hierarchy, elders are also ranked above the youth—and, tragically, men over women.

Youth learn from elders how to behave in the assembly and serve not the one but the many. Elders, in turn, defer to ancestors, who are wiser still and appear to them in dreams to nourish their decisions. In fact, the human assembly is just one among many other assemblies. Nagas are keen observers of animal behavior. They keep close track of tiger collectives, which they also conceptualize as constituting assemblies where some tigers have a more dominant voice than others. Tiger assemblies discuss matters like how to hunt and share the prey. Nagas also identify python collectives as assemblies, associated especially with rivers. Further, they assert that the ancestors and spirits also lead collective lives. There are designated sites—hills, trees, rocks—especially identified as their sites of habitation.

The Naga world is thus a multidimensional reality. In each dimension, on each plane—of humans, tigers, pythons, ancestors, spirits—life is lived in the collective, and decisions are taken through deliberation. These multiple assemblages also continually refract one another, like a play of mirrors. Tiger assemblies discuss human affairs; human assemblies discuss other types of animate beings. Human collectives traditionally honored and shared food with spirit (Ao Naga, *tsungrem*) collectives; humans and tigers sometimes share souls, creating a particularly strong interspecies bond; ancestors and other spirits communicate their wishes to humans. At the heart of Naga democracy is thus a dazzling matrix where each type of being lives and deliberates collectively, and all these different assemblies continually interact in what can perhaps be called, without too much exaggeration, a transbeing democracy.

> *Over and above these, the system of our Naga community organization, which is rooted in the humane principle of individual responsibility, sharing collectively the common weal and woe together, had stood the test of time without waver throughout those centuries of great changes.*

How then do we explain the grammar of the assembly, the syntax of agreement making, in the apparent absence of an abstraction called "community"? Our response would be: among the Naga, community is not a thing that exists a priori. Community is a process that emerges through the assemblies in the many dimensions. Community is never a thing that can be captured by a word—it is a perennial emergence. In earlier times, the human assemblies consisted of age groups, clans, and *khels*, and terminated at the village. (Tiger assemblies were more translocal.) However, over the past century, human assemblies have gradually evolved to also include village clusters, hill ranges, and tribes, all of which now manifest as autonomous assemblies that interlink in a continuous chain of public deliberation. Views and decisions must rise or be digested through these ranks, risking abortion at each level, to become rightful. Naga community is a surge of waves rather than a stable harbor.

> *We do not say that we have everything or do not need any other thing. That is sheer folly. But the important thing is we have all the basic needs in political matters, for country's administration, community organization, economic set-up (uki-ulie); and these institutions we have in the way we need it. These are not problems in Nagaland. It is not a grafted growth.*

Naga community is far from the "imagined community" theorized by Benedict Anderson. Though Phizo uses terms like "country," they are distant from any conception of the Naga community as a para-state nation. Relatedly, what he translates as "economic set-up" is not an abstraction like "the economy" or "the market," which arises from the exploitative interdependence created by capital. *Ukie-ulie* translates best as "our homes and fields."

Across the past half-century, the Indian state has climbed the Naga highlands, building an unprecedented infrastructure of top-down rule. In parallel, Christian conversion has steadily evacuated other-than-human beings from Naga assembly spaces. Nevertheless, all is not lost. Even today, many Naga clans, *khels*, and villages sit in assembly prior to the Indian state's official election day in order to deliberate their collective vote. This is an ontology poles apart from the Hegelian state's "I will," or indeed the will of the possessive individual of capitalism. Despite its flaws—above all, the subordination of women—the Naga assembly contains a majestic grammar of democracy that can transform our world, if the flaws can be overcome.

> *Our culture: a culture of love with a true respect*
> *for individual personality, a society that admits no*
> *strata of social class, caste, or creed, religion or race.*

When the Indian state failed to control the Naga uprising, it sought to co-opt, cajole, and arm those villages and clans whose assemblies had refused to join the Naga Army and made them fight on the state's behalf. When state-channeled development policies and projects collapsed, the state devolved all development initiatives and funds to the village assembly. When state frameworks of maintaining law and order unraveled, the state transferred most of its authority to customary laws and courts. And when the delivery of even basic state services collapsed in Nagaland, the lower bureaucracy was obliterated and all funds, authority, and responsibilities were

transferred to village assemblies. Community governance now takes care of education, health, electricity, and water. In all these spheres, Naga assemblies outperform the state. They offer real-life blueprints for a nonstate life. We do not need to create out of nothing a poststate future where collective deliberation has replaced state administration: it already exists here and now.

> *If our Naga civilization is not destroyed there is no possibility for any section of our people to become servile or entirely dependent on someone. [...] Need we stress it again how truly we love our native institutions of people's democracy where none is the master or servant but all are as parents and children, brothers and sisters.*

Being Shines in Subaltern Consciousness

Similar frameworks of conceptualizing community can be found in diverse forms across South Asia. Let us consider the Kabir tradition of northern India, a major inspiration for contemporary Dalit-Bahujan politics. Kabir was a lower-caste weaver raised in a Muslim family in fifteenth-century India. Songs attributed to him have circulated orally and in manuscript form across the centuries; many were collated by Kshitimohan Sen in the early twentieth century. Kabir is more than an individual—he is the sacred name of a subaltern epic.

For Kabir, the divine (*brahman*) and truth (*satya*) are present in all living beings (*jiv*). Hence, we must transcend the binary of "me" and "you" (*mai tai*, the Indian counterpart of *meum* and *tuum*) and regard all as a living being like ourself (*apna sa jiv sab ko janai*). We must destroy our egotism (*meri mamta*, literally, my mine-ness), caste arrogance (*jati abhiman*), caste ranks (*jati pangti*), discrimination of high and low (*uch nich*). We must be each other's habitations (*jiv ko jiv adhar*).

This standpoint leads to condemnation of Brahmanical caste discrimination and of conflicts between Hindus and Muslims. In the Kabir tradition, love (*prema*) and mercy (*daya*) should animate our relations with social others— hence the tradition criticizes animal killing. The belief that the same divine is present in all leads to a focus on *samata*—a word, cognate to "same," used in northern Indian languages to express an ethics of "equality." The tradition proclaims *samata* between women and men (*nari purush samatai ho*).

In the foothills of the Himalayas, we see comparable attitudes among the Rajavamshis, the largest Dalit community in West Bengal and one of India's most populous and well-organized peasant communities. Since the early twentieth century, Rajavamshis have theorized about *samaj*, translating this into English as "community" as well as "society." In his bilingual correspondence with the colonial state in 1917, Rajavamshi leader Panchanan Barma argued that the Rajavamshis had always been a "self-governing" (*atmashasani*) and "representative" *samaj*. When the British devolved powers to Indians, they should devolve them to communities like theirs who represented the majority of the population, rather than to elite Indians alone. Hence, "village Communities (*gramyasamiti*) and Panchayats" should be "the basis of popular representation." This led to an internationalist blueprint where the Rajavamshis aspired to be "loving confederates with all other similar Samajas as also the rest of mankind." This was, in germ, a vision of world governance through communities-in-association coexisting with states.

In their internal discussions, away from the prying eyes of the colonial state, Rajavamshi thinkers outlined an anarchist vision where rule by king (*rajar shasan*) and rule by community/society (*samajshasan*) would gradually be replaced by self-rule (*atmashasan*) and ultimately by the abolition of all government. In practice, Rajavamshis self-organized against high-caste social, economic, and political dominance, expanding their political influence and instantiating welfare measures for community members. They eroded many internal class and gender inequalities. Rajavamshis devised new techniques of caring for cattle, regarding them as part of their community. Through the Tebhaga sharecroppers' struggle of the 1940s, Rajavamshi men and women built an Indigenous communism.

In nearby Tripura, Indigenous shifting-cultivator communities used traditional forms of organization to build a socialist infrastructure of self-rule and territorial autonomy. Led by statesmen like Dasarath Deb, Tripuris have fought to secure their freedoms against a settler-colonial Indian state and high-caste Bengali elites. Traditional Tripuri political thought, as embodied in the precolonial chronicle *Rajmala*, advocated "nonviolence toward living beings" (*prani ahimsan*) and resistance to tyrants. Contemporary Tripuri thinkers like Bijay Debbarma and Arun Debbarma build their vision of Indigenous customary democracy by drawing on these traditions. Simultaneously, communist politics has influenced Tripuris to overcome ethnic, class, and gender inequalities.

These examples show that Indian subalterns have waged their most successful political and socioeconomic battles against colonial and postcolonial elites by drawing upon the organizational and intellectual resources of their communities while simultaneously eroding the class and gender inequalities within the communities.

Dalit-Bahujan-Adivasi-Indigenous communities have traditionally been more gender-egalitarian than high-caste communities. Hence Dalit women frequently relate their struggles to broader communitarian aspirations for freedom and dignity. In *Ami Keno Charal Likhi* (Why I Write "Untouchable"), the Namashudra-origin writer Kalyani Thakur Charal urges us to remember these caste movements often rooted in Dalit spirituality, such as Matua devotion and Baul minstrelsy.

Suraj Yengde observes: "Dalit spiritualism exists in variant forms across the Indian subcontinent. The remembrance of ancestors and devotion to their egalitarianism promote the healing of the deeply wounded Dalit community. [...] Dalit spiritualism is an in-practice phenomenon which goes beyond the narrow ideology of state secularism. Dalit spiritualism lives with a hope of the divine. The divine is pierced and cut across as hope. Kancha Ilaiah describes this as a lively culture of gods and goddesses wherein the spiritualism informs the metaphysics of Dalit and Shudra cultural production." In India, where caste segregates, the belief in common Being unites. It is the basis of solidarity for the oppressed against the oppressor, and has been so for centuries.

South Asian subaltern communities today establish ever-deeper solidarities spanning India and the world. In late nineteenth-century Maharashtra, Jyotirao Phule compared Brahmanical caste oppression of lower-caste Indians with the experience of American slavery as well as with European subjugation of the Native Americans. Today, Dalit thinkers draw upon B. R. Ambedkar's thought as well as on African American political philosophy and literature. Manohar Mouli Biswas thus sees the experience of Dalits and African Americans as comparable in the way that surplus value is extracted from the poor. He recognizes that caste- and race-based exploitation negate humanity. Many other Dalit thinker-activists connect the struggle against caste discrimination to the struggle against racism. Meanwhile, South Asian communities that had traditionally existed outside Brahmanical caste society—categorized by the Indian Constitution as Scheduled Tribes—have participated with vigor in sessions of the United Nations Working Group on Indigenous Populations. Today, the category of indigeneity finds significant traction in subaltern public spheres.

Those who destroy nonhuman worlds in contemporary India are mainly high-caste functionaries of state and capital, or an elite stratum of Dalit-Bahujan-Adivasi-Indigenous politicians and capitalists who serve as subordinate collaborators of the high-caste ruling classes. Those protecting nonhuman worlds are mainly non-elite Dalit-Bahujan-Adivasi-Indigenous actors: peasants, pastoralists, and forest-dependent groups for whom kinship with the nonhuman is lived reality. Kalyani Thakur Charal's description of named cows "who were members of our family, like our brothers and sisters"—her fond remembrance of the conjugal lives of goats, ducks, and hens—is emblematic of subaltern care for the nonhuman.

Flashpoints like Singur, Nandigram, and Niyamgiri represent confrontations between these two poles. Hence, no ecological politics that ignores questions of caste and indigeneity will be successful in India. When subaltern Indians self-organize pan-subcontinental and transnational solidarities, they are inaugurating a new political economy. They connect the regional to the planetary, bypassing and eroding the monopolistic sovereignty claimed by the nation-state, which, as Yengde notes, "is in any case used by the ruling class to enjoy the inherited privileges of caste society." To protect soil, water, air, plants, and animals from state-aided capital, we must uphold this politics. If states persist, they may be allowed to exist as just one political level among many, and then not the most important one that can block substate and transnational organizing.

India already possesses a rich infrastructure of Dalit-Bahujan parties that have galvanized millions of people from small villages to the largest of cities, and from time to time formed governments. Other regional parties have also often prioritized welfarist redistribution over capitalist growth. Together, they offer a readily available infrastructure that can be turned against the nexus of right-wing nationalism and necropolitical capitalism that governs India today—where any opposition to capitalism is labeled antidevelopment and antinational. When the opponents are minorities, like the Muslims of Kashmir and of the Lakshadweep Islands, they are more readily pulverized.

Subaltern Studies 2.0 advocates alliance between these parties and global ecological politics: it urges a political education and mobilization nourished by their symbiosis in order to fight high-caste state and capital. After all, most Indian victims of climate change—from peasants committing suicide because of drought and crop failure to migrant laborers in the Middle East dying of heat stress—are Dalit-Bahujan-Adivasi-Indigenous multitudes. It is they who create value for capitalism, and who first die from it: from coal miners contracting lung diseases in eastern India to cleaners dying from exposure to toxic waste in Delhi.

Against Possessive Man, Being!

Latin America offers us role models. Marisol de la Cadena shows how the indigenous communities of Peru recognize mountains, rivers, and lagoons as *tirakuna*, a Quechua term signifying earth beings. *Ayllu* embodies the nondifference of being and place: a relationality of interdependence between human and nonhuman beings that animates struggles against white settler landlords and extractivist states in the Andes. Thea Riofrancos describes similar struggles in Ecuador against private capitalist and state capitalist extractivism. Communitarian solidarities are at the heart of a new internationalism in Latin America. De la Cadena, Mario Blaser, and Arturo Escobar see this as the rise of Indigenous political ontologies and world making against capitalist globalization.

The *jiv* of the Kabir tradition, the *prani* of Tripura, the *tirakuna* of Peru—these variously express a fundamental commitment to Being. The state demands commitment to sovereign power; capital demands commitment to profit. Many, perhaps most, human societies emphasize binding commitments to human and other-than-human beings with whom we live in community. Today we need to recommit ourselves to Being. We must negate our desires for individual growth at the cost of the many.

Difference-into-Unity!

Whether we admit this or not, we are connected. Deleuze and Guattari may deny the root, complicate the unity—but their very conceptualization of that which connects beings reveals the possibility of connection, and hence of a substrate that underlies plurality. When they exemplify the rhizome in a pack of animals, they affirm that which makes the pack possible, a Being-consciousness that bonds beings. What began as a multiplicity shows itself in dialectical reversal to be a connected unity. The logic of difference reverses, overcomes, and sublates itself into a logic of interdependence, or better, an *achintyabhedabheda* between singularity and plurality, unity and difference. Beings are separate and yet connected, in union, as Being. All radical politics depends upon recognizing this rootedness of Beings in Being. We are Indra's net, where each jewel node of the net reflects and manifests all the others. To deny this fundamental connection is not to negate it but to obscure ourselves. Being is interdependence. Being is that which connects, the very possibility of connection.

Actually existing communities function as proto-states or para-states when they restrict the decision—the "I will" of Hegel—to specific sections, generally men of power. A community is then already on the way to becoming a state. Becoming community involves reversing this: opening speech, debate, mutuality of decision to the multitudes. The community is the common; *samaj* is establishing the *sama*—no high and low. It is the space where beings share Being in common.

Being a World for Others

Philippe Descola's *Beyond Nature and Culture* catalogues how diverse communities, from South America to Aboriginal Australia, connect beings. World-making is making *samaj* between humans and other-than-humans. The *Brihadaranyaka Upanishad* is unequivocal—we are a world (*loka*) for all beings. In Patrick Olivelle's translation, when the self (*atman*) "provides food and shelter to human beings, he becomes thereby a world for human beings. When he procures fodder and water for livestock, he becomes thereby a world for livestock. When creatures, from wild animals and birds down to the very ants, find shelter in his houses, he becomes thereby a world for them. Just as a man desires the well-being of his own world, so all beings desire the well-being of anyone who knows this."

Interestingly, the Upanishads often attribute these discourses on interdependence of beings to subalterns, such as Raikva, a poor cart driver, and Satyakama Jabala, a servant woman's son of uncertain paternity; and non-human animals like wild geese and cattle. Brahmanical censorship has not succeeded in completely erasing the subaltern sources of Indian philosophy. Indeed, across the centuries in South Asia, Dalit-Bahujan-Adivasi-Indigenous peoples have affirmed divine immanence in all beings. From these communities have risen philosophers of Being—like Chokhamela, Kabir, Ravidas, and Tukaram.

These forms of interdependence are still alive today in South Asia. Ethnographic observation shows how, in the Bhutan highlands, herders refer to yaks as parents, siblings, or children, even as this attachment is also asymmetrical. They regulate their behavior to yak kin through norms of love, labor, and sometimes dislike, comparable to how they would relate to human kin. In return, yaks apply their senses (herders say *wangpo*, a Tibetan Buddhist word, used as equivalent of Sanskrit *indriya*) and memory (*lokshay*) to distinguish between strange and familiar humans. Yaks recognize humans through their gender, age, and personality traits. They cultivate unique and stable relations with each such human being. In Bhutanese understanding, yaks and humans reincarnate in each other's realms. Further, yaks herd humans in one era, and humans herd yaks in another. Human and yak gestures converge during rituals for propitiating territorial gods. The gods in turn ensure the well-being of humans and yaks, as well as the lands, lakes, and streams where they both pasture.

Animals: Primal Instructors of Humans

While living together, humans draw lessons from animal social organization. Biologists have observed that cranes habitually form monogamous unions that often last a lifetime. These are maintained through intimate unison calls, joint nesting, and coparenting. Some cranes divorce, mostly on account of unsuccessful breeding attempts. In Bhutan, many folktales and songs center on love, commitment, and heartbreak among cranes. Humans regularly perform these narratives through ritual dances. Cranes are role models for stable marriage and sexual fidelity. The Indian ornithologist Salim Ali notes that since sarus cranes "pair for life," "their devotion to each other has earned them a degree of popular sentiment amounting to sanctity" across South Asia. "They are zealously protected by the inhabitants in many parts with the result that the birds become tame and confiding."

This forces us to radically rethink our theories about the origins of marriage and kinship. Anthropological studies on the origin and evolution of marriage—the incest taboo or alliance theory, totemism or private property—have remained largely anthropocentric. In contrast, we argue that it is quite plausible that humans saw animals as role models for organizing their social behavior. That is, humans did not invent marriage and sexual fidelity sui generis, but rather emulated the behavior of select animals, cranes among them, with whom they came to co-inhabit territory.

Human sensibilities about ritual have also been reinforced by animal behavior. Across the Hindu-Buddhist world, circumambulation (Sanskrit, *pradakshina, parikrama*) is a sacred movement that emulates the east-to-west movement of the sun. Its roots lie in ancient Indo-European rituals that shaped human migrations across Eurasia and left traces in South Asian as well as Roman ritual. But humans are, of course, not the only migrating animals. Birds also migrate, using the sun to orient themselves, much like ancient humans; they also navigate with the help of physical landmarks. In Bhutan, the Phobjikha Valley is the winter residence of migratory black-necked cranes. They use the mountaintop monastery as a landmark to navigate their altitude and flight pattern by circling around it multiple times before landing in the marsh valley. They repeat this during their departure to Tibet in early spring. The Bhutanese notice this similarity between human and crane circumambulation around the monastery. Hence they refer to the cranes as *lhab bja*, heavenly birds, believing them to be bodhisattvas, wisdom beings: a sacralized acknowledgment of crane intelligence. Human rituals, especially crane dances, have evolved to represent these convergences between human and crane movements.

Humans also learn ethical conduct from animals. Vultures across the world are obligate scavengers. They refuse to hunt or kill living beings—those whom the Bhutanese call *semchen* (sentient being). For the

Bhutanese, this refusal to kill beings that have a mind (*sem*) exhibits a spiritual consciousness—it resonates with the Buddhist prohibition on killing (*sok chay kak dham*). In reciprocation, the Bhutanese offer human corpses to the vultures through sky burials, also obviating the need for cremation and burial in a landscape where timber and suitable land are both scarce. They invoke vultures as role models of nonviolence; this is one source for the widespread Bhutanese resistance to slaughterhouses that kill *semchen*. They revere vultures as spiritual practitioners (male, *pow*; female, *pamo*). Many Bhutanese believe that vultures distinguish during sky burials between the bones of good human beings, which are immediately consumed, and those of bad people, which are not eaten or eaten only reluctantly. Vultures are glorified as karmic judges, umpires in the cycle of rebirth.

In the Americas too, humans are shaped by animal behavior. Eduardo Kohn shows how among the Runa in Ecuador's Upper Amazon, humans, spirits, jaguars, and dogs represent each other, make worlds for each other. Eduardo Viveiros de Castro describes an Amazonia where humans, plants, animals, and spirits are equally persons, differing only in their bodies. Irving Hallowell writes about the Ojibwa people of Canada, who recognize nonhumans like bears and thunderbirds as intelligent beings one can converse with. Animal spirits warn Davi Kopenawa and other Yanomami shamans in Brazil about the dangers brought by white men.

The Light of Being-Consciousness

This is Being-consciousness. Human and nonhuman beings cothink and co-create each other's worlds. The *Maha Upanishad* observes, *vasudhaiva kutumbakam*, the world is kin. Kin ties can be extended even to beings that threaten. In West Papua, Sophie Chao shows, the Indigenous Marind initially denied kinship ties to African oil palms, seeing them as embodiments of a brutal plantation capitalism, but later connected with them by recognizing that these plants had also been victimized by capital.

Humans have traditionally recognized other beings as beings, as persons, as kin. Of course, human society would not have been possible without some form of cothinking and corecognition between human and nonhuman beings. Domestication of animals is premised on animals distinguishing between their herdsmen/owners and strangers. Humans recognize that cattle, cats, and dogs can do this, modifying their behavior according to degrees of familiarity. The Roman who wrote *cave canem* knew that a dog can differentiate between his (and his human kin's) territory and another's. Roman law distinguished wild animals like pigeons, bees, and deer who habitually returned to human owners; wild animals who did not; and domestic animals like dogs and geese. Laws about human ownership of nonhuman animals were devised accordingly, based on differences in animal will and conduct. Human territoriality evolved from animal territorialities.

Kresimir Vukovic argues that Indo-European language speakers followed horses in spreading from the Central Asian steppes across Eurasia. He interprets rituals like the Indian Ashvamedha and the Roman Equus October as evidence of how horse-human collectives moved into new territories.

Humans have often watched and emulated animal behavior. Vukovic's research on the Roman Lupercalia festival shows that the festival was originally a rite of passage in which groups of human males identified with and mimicked wolf packs. The *Mundaka Upanishad* observes the friendship that exists between birds and uses it as a role model to think philosophically about the relations between selves.

Human mastery over nonhuman beings is premised on a double move, of recognition and disavowal: recognition that humans can indeed communicate with dogs, cattle, birds, horses, etc. and a simultaneous negation of nonhuman beings as thinking and communicating beings. Even Derrida, in *The Animal That Therefore I Am*, hesitates to recognize that the animal can speak: "It would not be a matter of 'giving speech back' to animals." In his view, rather than thinking that humans have special access to Being as such—a capacity denied to animals in modern European thinking—it is more productive to question the possibility of this access even for humans.

In contrast, we assert that language, speech, is central to the interspecies interdependence that constitutes Being, that establishes communication between beings. To insist that nonhuman beings can think and speak is not anthropocentrism—it is a reversal of the vulgar anthropocentrism that denies full beingness to nonhumans. It is to expand our understanding of what counts as speech by drawing upon many—perhaps most—human societies that have traditionally recognized this. After all, given that humans have evolved from primates, where do we draw the entirely arbitrary line and say: until here are animals who cannot think and speak, and from here are humans who can do both?

Once When Animals Could Speak

Human denial of speech to animals has become universal only with the globalization of capitalism. In South Asia, the *Rigveda* (mid-late second millennium BCE) observed (in Stephanie Jamison's translation) that "beasts of all forms speak (*vadanti*) her"—"her" referring to *vach*, speech personified as a goddess. Bharata's *Natyashastra* (late first millennium BCE/early first millennium CE), a celebrated treatise on the performing arts, recognizes "other-origin language" (*yonyantaribhasha*) as a category alongside Sanskrit and regional human languages that could be used in theater. This included languages that arose from domestic and wild animals (*gramyaranyapashudbhava*) and various birds (*nanavihangaja*).

In *On the Intelligence of Animals*, Plutarch invokes the ability of some birds to be trained to talk, to suggest that animals possessed *prophorikos logos*, uttered word/reason. He cites Aristotle on how birds teach songs to their children. And finally, the fact that a bird could sometimes train itself, without human aid, to imitate new sounds showed an even greater reason (*logikōteran*). By contrast, Descartes observes in *Discourse on the Method*: "nor must it be thought, like some of the ancients, that the beasts speak (*que les bêtes parlent*), although we do not understand their language." Capitalist modernity expropriated animals of speech in a great act of primitive accumulation.

Subaltern Studies 2.0 urges a return to what humanity has always known and is confirmed today by the natural sciences. Thom van Dooren shows how crows can recognize the individuality of beings, including of other crows and humans; make friends and give gifts; distinguish between fair and unfair behavior; use fire and innovate tools; grieve for the dead. Hal Whitehead and Luke Rendell show how whales transmit songs and dolphins whistles; both have a keen sense of morality and display intra- as well as interspecies cooperation. Dolphins exhibit their condemnation of human behavior they consider as socially wrong. Like bonobos and some parrots, they can understand basic syntax.

The study of "animal culture" is a flourishing field today, as are ever-growing paradigms like "animal personhood," "plant kinship," "multispecies becoming," "earth Animism," and "ecologies of relations." These advances in scholarship have practical implications. For example, a group of British Members of Parliament recently urged that octopuses and lobsters be legally protected from suffering, where possible, given that they have feelings and sentience. Scholars have also started recognizing that plants can identify and prefer their kin during feeding and warn them against insect invasion. There is growing awareness of plant cooperation and communication. Ellison Banks Findly underlines how in the ancient Buddhist *Vinaya* and *Nikaya* texts, the recognition that plants are living and sentient beings went hand in hand with restrictions on felling trees. We hope that recent scientific discoveries will have comparable ramifications for protecting plant beingness.

Animal Democracy: The World's Oldest Polities

Recent scientific research has highlighted how many animals—from bees to horses, bison, deer, elephants, and species of birds and fish—practice collective decision making. Decision making is not the monopoly of the dominant; a broad multitude express their opinions, "voting" on such key issues as where the pack should go in search of food, what activities the group will engage in, where their new habitation will be, and who will be the new leader. The leaders can be overruled by the majority. The term "animal democracy" has been used in a recent Arte documentary film, directed by Emma Baus, to categorize these processes. Such knowledge is gradually entering the broader public sphere. A 2020 article in the newspaper *The*

Guardian, by Paola Rosa-Aquino, was titled: "Animals vote, too: how different species choose—or depose—a leader." The article focused on voting among honeybees, Indian jumping ants, and pigeons.

In parallel, political theorists have started arguing that animals should be recognized as political actors. Sue Donaldson and Will Kymlicka suggest that domesticated animals should be acknowledged as cocitizens, free-living animals in the wilderness, autonomous beings exercising sovereignty in their territories, and nondomesticated free-living animals in urban and suburban regions recognized as denizens among us. Criticizing the anthropocentric nature of modern-Western political theory, they advance the vision of a multispecies zoopolis.

There are older intellectual traditions that recognize animals as political beings. Humans have long been aware of animal politics, including animal democracy. The *Jataka* stories, which date to late first millennium BCE/early first millennium CE India, offer a classic case. In the Pali version of the *Tittira* (Partridge) *Jataka*, the Buddha speaks about animals who were initially *asabhagavuttino* but later, after deliberation, became *sabhagavuttino*. Pali expert Stefan Baums points out to us in personal communication that the term *sabhagavuttino* can be interpreted in two ways: as "going into an assembly" or "having a shared life." Modern translators generally opt for the second meaning. In either case, it is clear that animals form a community through deliberation. Further, the Buddha, according to this story, takes the animal community as a role model for his *sangha*. Monks are advised to cooperate with each other and accord respect to seniors, as do animals.

The *Pali Mahasutasomajataka* observes that all (*sabbe*) the sea fish came to a unanimity of will (*ekachhanda*) in order to select a ruler, after observing that bipeds and quadrupeds (*dipadachatuppadanam*) have rulers. The story hints at the possibility of interspecies learning effects in organizing collectives.

Human observation of animal politics has often been driven by political needs. This is transparent when it comes to animals like elephants and horses that have been central to state building. India's most famous manual of statecraft, Kautilya's *Arthashastra* (late first millennium BCE/early first millennium CE), describes at great length the management of elephant forests and elephant social behavior, as (in Olivelle's translation) a "king's victory is led by elephants." Hence the state should maintain an entire human bureaucracy around elephants that, among other things, "should keep a written record" of social structures: "those moving in herds, those roaming alone, those driven from a herd, and the leaders of herds." Understanding the political functioning of elephant collectives (*yutha*)—from identifying the leader of the collective (*yuthapati*) to identifying the one expelled from the collective (*niryutha*)—lay at the heart of human monarchic military state building.

The Sanskrit text even equates techniques of controlling elephants and controlling kings. Kautilya advises that people in an enemy state should be turned against their king by suggesting to them that a king who kills people is like "an elephant blinded by intoxication" (*madandho hasti*). "It is possible to liquidate him by instigating a rival elephant."

Despite colonialism, Indians never completely forgot these ancient traditions. During the late-nineteenth and early twentieth century, anticolonial Indian intellectuals sometimes used models of animal democracy to condemn the colonial state and call for democratization among humans. In "Hanumadbabu Samvad," Bankimchandra Chattopadhyay contrasts the genuine freedom enjoyed by monkeys to the fake liberties and limited local self-government the British offered to Indians. The monkey god Hanuman lampoons Westernized Indian elites for mistaking these political sops as liberty. Instead, as a monkey, he can declare: "There is no government among us except self-rule (*atmashasan*). We are a free nation (*svadhin jati*) on earth." In "Majantali Sarkar," Upendra Kishore Roychowdhury contrasted the freedom enjoyed by forest animals to the tax-hungry human state.

In his interwar novel *The Chief of the Herd/Yuthapati*, Dhan Gopal Mukerji describes forms of election of leaders, political communication, and consensus building among wild elephants, as well as cooperation between elephants and other forest animals and collective resistance to humans. The novel stemmed from a broader Indian nationalist discourse stating that processes of democratic deliberation and collective decision making could be found in many societies. These traditions were not unique to European societies, as the British claimed. In contemporaneous Europe, anarchist thinkers sometimes referenced animal politics to similarly emphasize the universality of democracy. Peter Kropotkin's *Mutual Aid* exemplifies this. It describes variegated forms of social organization, solidarity, and cooperation among numerous bird, insect, and mammal species.

The First Imperialism: Human Colonization of Animal Polities

Textual and ethnographic evidence from South Asia impels us to argue that domestication of animals ricocheted back to monarchize human politics. If we define colonialism as a form of systematic exploitation that invades and subordinates another political system and legitimates this conquest through ideology, then the first colonialism that human beings perpetrated was undoubtedly over the animal world. The first anticolonial resistance was waged by animals. The *Shatapatha Brahmana*, an early first-millennium BCE Sanskrit text, records that the gods wanted to subjugate animals (*pashu*). The animals offered resistance; they "wished to go away." In Julius Eggeling's translation, "animals did not at first submit thereto that they should become food." They thought about the gods: "It is to be feared lest they, being exhausted, may hurt us: how, indeed, will they deal with us?" The gods then threatened the animals with the thunderbolt. They also tempted the animals with the promise of a home (*griha*), represented by the householder's fire (*garhapatya*).

Domestication certainly involved both coercion and allure. Subsequently, similar techniques of domestication were applied on humans themselves. The *Atharva Veda*, another early first-millennium BCE Sanskrit text, calls the human king *ekavrisha*, the one/sole (*eka*) bull (*vrisha*). It prays to Indra, the leader of the gods, that enemies of the king be emasculated (to adopt Maurice Bloomfield's translation of *nirakshnuhi*, juxtaposed with William Whitney's translation, "unman," and Albrecht Weber's argument that the word is comparable to *nirashta*); that heaven and earth become the king's cows; that cattle and other animals shall become fond of the king. We can compare this to a hymn of the *Rigveda*, where Indra is described as a bull (*vrisha*) fighting against castrated (*nirashta*) bullocks and defeating them. According to Michael Witzel, Vedic texts of this era reflect state formation in early South Asia, and especially the birth of the Kuru polity. We would underscore that a technique of animal domestication—reducing rivalry between male bulls by emasculating all except one—was applied to monarchize human politics. The human monarch, like the divine king Indra, was shaped on the model of the bull, with the subjects taking the place of the cows and castrated bullocks.

In the most famous Indian narrative about the origin of the state, retold in Sanskrit and regional languages for two millennia, the first "good" king, Prithu, milked—in some versions, by threatening to hunt down—the Earth, who had taken the form of a cow, to get the earth's produce for his subjects. The state was born by domesticating the bovinized earth. Human colonialism of the animal world had given birth to human self-colonization, that is, to the state. This state was multispecies patriarchy; the monarch, the sole phallus. In *Classifying the Universe*, Brian Smith shows how Brahmin authors—who sought state patronage—suggested repeatedly that the subjects were like food for the rulers. They also compared the subjects to domesticated animals and plants.

In Bhutan too, control of animal polities has been central to human state building. The seventeenth-century black-slate Edict of Punakha Dzong, described by its cotranslator, Michaela Windischgraetz, as Bhutan's first constitution, notes that the state should take care of the uteruses of female yaks. This phrasing makes sense if we bring it into dialogue with ethnography. In contemporary Bhutan, the *zholu* or bull leader—who would normally be in charge of the herd—is exiled. (The animal world is full of Napoleons in Elba.) Considered too wild, he is only allowed to return to the herd once a year, for mating; he retains the vestige of sovereignty in being exempted from all labor. Humans deal more summarily with other bulls by castrating them around the age of three or four years. Humans have thus monarchized yak politics, removing potential conflicts for power.

In colonial India, the British would generally support one native prince against other contenders for the throne in a princely state. By removing rival centers of power, concentrating sovereignty in one prince, and then subjecting him to British control, the colonial state monarchized human governance and created a monistic and absolutist structure of state sovereignty. But the basic template for this is older—it derives from human colonialism of the animal world.

In this light, we can better interpret colonialism as involving multispecies imperialism. As Jules Skotnes-Brown has argued in relation to Africa, European colonizers implemented remarkably similar strategies to domesticate, "civilize," and territorially confine both Indigenous humans and nonhuman animals like elephants.

In Bhutan, humans choose the leader from the young yaks based on physical features, such as longer legs, brighter color, and larger size—and castrate the rest. The castrated bulls are then used in transportation and agriculture. The herd of female yaks is entrusted to the human yak herder, who traditionally offered part of the yak produce to the state and monasteries. Thus the herder is the original stranger king who colonizes the animal world by arbitrarily selecting and then exiling the indigenous animal leader, taking his place, and castrating half of the herd. The human state takes on the herdsman's stranger-king function on a more macrocosmic level through its legal framework of tribute extraction. Humans also claim to speak on behalf of the yaks to the gods. Marshall Sahlins identified stranger kings as founders of human states. In fact, domestication constitutes the first exercise of stranger king colonialism. Scientific research confirms that humans manipulated dominance hierarchies among select animal species to insert themselves at the top of those hierarchies.

Decolonize Animal Polities!

Today, however, owing to industrial capitalism, human colonialism of the animal world has become genocidal—it is no more a traditional monarchy. In the modern dairy industry, male cattle are often slaughtered at a young age rather than emasculated, with females allowed to survive for their milk-producing capacity. Seven billion male chicks are slaughtered annually because they do not lay eggs. Female ducks are often killed because they are less useful than males in foie gras production. No decolonization shall be complete until this genocidal imperialism, this highest stage of capitalism, is overthrown.

If we are to end this state of extermination in which a large number of animal species live today, we have to recognize animals as part of an interspecies legal order, a more-than-human demos. We can learn here from several societies, past and present. For example, classical Indian political thought is saturated with laws of interspecies relations. In the *Arthashastra*, state legislation protects elephants: the punishment for a human killing an elephant is death. In the *Chandimangal* tradition, composed in several versions in Bengal between the sixteenth and eighteenth centuries, animals of the forest are seen as composing a society. In the late sixteenth/early seventeenth-century version by Mukunda, forest animals petition the goddess Chandi, herself part animal, to transform them from a condition of perennial fear (*sadai sashanka*) to a state of nonfear (*niratanka*). In response, Chandi organizes the animals into a polity, a sort of constitutional monarchy, laying down laws of interspecies behavior and restrictions on indiscriminate killing. Mukunda emphasizes the framework of nonconflict (*avirodha*) that Chandi institutes between specific animals. As the goddess removes their fear by giving them rules, the text calls her Abhaya, the Fear Remover. We can see her as a personification of the animal polity, an embodiment of the laws that govern conduct between different species: a multispecies demos.

In Sanskrit, the word *samaj* denotes alike the community/society of animals and that of humans, a tradition that continues in modern Indian languages. For example, in contemporary Bengali, the term *pashusamaj*—community/society of animals—remains in common usage. The same applies for terms for leadership, like *pati*, and collectivity, such as *yutha*, *kula*, and *dala*, traditionally and still applied to describe both human and animal political societies in India. Unlike in modern English, in which terms like "herd," "pack," and "flock" are normally reserved for animals and only disparagingly or ironically used for humans, the great divide between humans and animals has not taken place. There is no linguistic sense that animals have a different social form than humans.

Humans have always known that animals have their polity, even collective deliberation and decision making, as do humans. For Greeks writing in the Athenian polis, it was obvious to reflect about animal species whose organization seemed most akin to theirs. In *Phaedo*, Plato praises bees, wasps, and ants as political species (*politikon genos*), reincarnations of souls that practiced moderation and justice. They are role models of virtue. Aristotle, in *History of Animals*, sees man, bee, wasp, ant, and crane as political creatures (*politika*). He distinguishes between those animals, like cranes and bees, who submit to a ruler (*uph' hegemona*) and those, like ants, not subject to any governance (*anarkha*).

Polybius, writing in the world of the Hellenistic monarchies, observed in his *Histories* that animals like bulls, goats, and cocks accepted the leadership of the strongest among them. He thought that humans also tended to gravitate toward this model of monarchy (*monarkhia*), culminating finally in kingship (*basileia*). Later, writing in the aftermath of civil wars that had torn Rome apart, Virgil in *Georgics* described how bees constitute a *gens*, organized into peoples (*populi*) and living under laws (*sub legibus aevum*); they share in divine intelligence (*partem divinae mentis*).

Virgil admired the division of labor among bees, as well as their respectful disposal of the dead—a process that has attracted modern scientific research and is categorized by Virgil as involving sad funerals (*tristia funera*). Bees were supposedly more loyal to their leaders than many human peoples. In their internecine conflicts, the wills of the common people (*animi vulgi*) played a central role. The poet instructs humans to observe and intervene in bee political organization, for example, by supporting the stronger bee leader (*ductor*) against the weaker. Observing bees will thus make humans efficient beekeepers, as well as indirectly impart political virtues.

To deal effectively with animals, humans have for millennia keenly observed their politics and democracy. Without such observation, humans would not have become efficient beekeepers, cattle herders, shepherds, mahouts, stable hands, and fishermen. Given the importance of animals like cattle, horses, and elephants in human polities, we can go a step further and say: humans and animals have co-created polities. The demos, the *samaj*, emerges through political negotiation between human polities and animal polities. Texts like the *Jatakas*, Kautilya's *Arthashastra*, and Virgil's *Georgics* are just famous examples of much wider worldviews, where animal polities are observed both to draw lessons about organizing human conduct and to exploit the polities for human gain—tame elephants, extract honey, and so on. Humans manipulate animal polities just as they manipulate other human polities, in a complex game of interspecies international relations. As in any politics, there are stark inequalities of power, but also intimacy and dependence.

In modern times, scientists have gone much beyond the Buddha, Kautilya, Plato, or Virgil in empirically demonstrating animal politics. Simultaneously, the industrialization of animal use has ensured that animal politics has fallen out of the general human common sense. When we buy animal products in the supermarket, we do not think that these are the detritus of industrialized extermination of political actors; that we are assassinating voters, waging genocide against democracies. A supermarket is a morgue. Capitalism transforms animals from political actors to commodities, sending to the slaughterhouse of oblivion at least three millennia of human thought. Wild animals that cannot be commodified are dismissed as vermin. Only in this landscape can the political be thought of as a human monopoly, a transition from animal nature to human polity. The *Jataka* is then regarded as fable, Virgil reduced to a work of literature. Species reality becomes myth.

Multibeing Demos, Constitution to Come

In this long light, we can better contextualize recent developments in restoring personhood to nonhuman beings. In 2017, Maori agitation led to the New Zealand Parliament passing an act recognizing Te Awa Tupua—defined as "an indivisible and living whole, comprising the Whanganui River from the mountains to the sea, incorporating all its physical and metaphysical elements"—as a legal person with rights. The river embodies the sacred ancestry and being of many Maoris; hence the act underlines "the inseparability of the people and the River." Similar legal personality has also been accorded to Te Urewera and Mount Taranaki. In 2018, the Supreme Court of Colombia recognized the Colombian Amazon as an "entity" (*entidad*), a "subject of rights." These are unevenly successful attempts to overcome white settler-colonial capitalism and translate ancient cosmopolitics into a modern Western constitutional language.

From recognizing the personhood, the legal subjectivity, of specific beings it is but a step to a larger revolution: giving legal recognition to the interdependence between beings, to Being-in-common. The "rights of nature" enshrined in the 2008 Constitution of Ecuador are nourished by the Indigenous Quechua perspective of *sumak kawsay*, rendered into Spanish as *buen vivir*. The constitution endows rights to maternal Earth, revered as Pacha Mama. In 2010, Bolivia passed the Law of the Rights of Mother Earth, underlining "the community of beings which comprise Mother Earth" (*la comunidad de seres que componen la Madre Tierra*). That same year, a Universal Declaration of Rights of Mother Earth was proclaimed in Bolivia by the World People's Conference on Climate Change and the Rights of Mother Earth. It declared that "Mother Earth is a living being," "a unique, indivisible, self-regulating community of interrelated beings that sustains, contains and reproduces all beings." Here "each being is defined by its relationships as an integral part of Mother Earth." The term "being" was defined as including "ecosystems, natural communities, species and all other natural entities which exist as part of Mother Earth."

In these documents, "being" includes both biotic and abiotic beings. In many parts of the world, the relations of interdependence between biotic and abiotic beings—in modern parlance, ecosystems—are personified as deities. These include rivers, lakes, fields, forests, mountains, pluvial movements, and telluric currents. These deities are propitiated as territorial gods and spirits. They are often cast as the original landowners, protectors, and providers. Humans are not allowed to damage or destroy them with impunity. They have to relate to them through mediators—shamans and prophets—as well as covenants.

For many societies, the interdependence of all terrestrial beings, biotic and abiotic, is itself a person. For example, Indians have long worshipped the goddess Prithivi or Bhudevi. During the anticolonial struggle, Indian thinkers like Rabindranath Tagore spoke on behalf of this personified Earth against the empire of capital. In more recent times, Bruno Latour speaks of Gaia as possessed of majesty. "To live in the epoch of the Anthropocene is to acknowledge a strange and difficult *limitation of powers* in favor of Gaia." Climate change, an imbalance in the relation between biotic and abiotic beings, thus represents chaos in the world of gods as well as of men. Environmental humanities is necessarily environmental theology: a way of inviting back exiled beings and balances as kin, comrade, and deity.

Karma Ura notes that in Bhutan, "*Nas dag, zhi dag* and *yulha* are immortal owners or landlords," while humans manifest as "ephemeral travelers passing through their territory." Humans offer these gods *serkem* (alcohol), *sang* (incense), *lungta* (prayer), and supplication rituals. Humans must ask the deities for permission to settle, cultivate, and flourish in their lands. Without divine consent, farming, damming, tunneling, mining, and construction of houses and roads remains illegitimate. To avoid divine wrath, negotiations are undertaken, sometimes grudgingly, by planners, investors, contractors, and builders.

Alongside this original political society in Bhutan, nourishing it, exists an elaborate grammar of norms that draws on Sanskritic and Tibetan Buddhism. This comprises moral norm (phonetic Dzongkha, *cho*; Tibetan *chos*; Sanskrit, *dharma*) and law (phonetic Dzongkha, *thim*; Tibetan, *khrims*; Sanskrit, *shila*, including the *panchashila*). Desire realm beings (*'dod khamspa*) are expected to limit their desires in order to escape the desire realm (*'dod khams*; Sanskrit, *kamadhatu*). These norms draw in part on premodern and modern state laws but cannot be reduced to them. The premodern state in Bhutan, like premodern states elsewhere, extracted labor and resources through tributary hierarchies. The modern state in Bhutan, like modern states elsewhere, often enforces biopolitical governance. But the norm world we are discussing exceeds these institutions of domination. Ethnography reveals its tenacious persistence, particularly among subaltern rural communities. It is manifested in nonviolence toward living beings, resistance to elite-modern introduction of slaughterhouses, the veneration of nonhuman animals, the reluctance to drastically modify landscapes.

In Pali and Sanskrit Buddhist texts of ancient India, like the *Sutta Pitaka* and the *Lalitavistara*, *dharma* norms aimed at *bahujanahitaya bahujanasukhaya*, the welfare (*hita*) of many beings (*bahujana*), the happiness (*sukha*) of many beings. Transmitted through Tibetan and Bhutanese codes, this inspires traditional Bhutanese political theory about the public promotion of happiness (phonetic Dzongkha, *ga-ki*; Tibetan *dga'a-skyid*; Sanskrit, *ananda, sukha*). The modern Bhutanese state has drawn on this framework to promote Gross National Happiness against capitalist Gross Domestic Product. Bhutan's constitution mandates that "a minimum of sixty percent of Bhutan's total land shall be maintained under forest cover for all time." Bhutan and Suriname are the only carbon-negative countries in the world today.

If we focus on Bhutanese norm worlds—especially as present among subaltern actors who can be studied through ethnography—we unearth the fascinating template of a more-than-human demos, based on relations between beings and norms. Hence Sahlins's thesis requires tempering. The original political society in Bhutan is not exclusively based on metapersons exerting sovereignty and owning means of production. It is not a despotism exercised by more-than-human beings. It embraces norms that promote public happiness and welfare and is enunciated through restrictions on possessive individualism. Metapersons and humans are alike subject to these laws.

Return, Ancient Constitution: What Was, Shall Again Be!

We may call this an ancient cosmic constitution. It encourages us to devise the future constitution of a more-than-human demos, a parliament of beings where the agency and welfare of nonhuman beings are given recognition alongside those of humans. Self-restriction of desire is designed here to limit production and consumption; it enables degrowth. This ancient and living constitution prohibits untrammelled slaughter of animals and plants, the destruction of ecosystems—those indispensable building blocks of capitalism.

When nineteenth- and early twentieth-century Europeans theorized about religion in relation to society,

Christianity was uppermost in their mind, particularly in its modern form, as accomplice of confessional state building, colonialism, and counter-revolution. Hence Ludwig Feuerbach saw religion as alienation of man's humanity to God. In reappropriating humanity, he denounced and exiled the animal from the ethical sphere. Following in that trail, Marx saw religion as an effect of ruling class domination, a mark of human wretchedness; Durkheim, as the point where human society recognized itself in the shape and name of the divine. None of them took nonhuman sentient beings seriously as norm-constituting actors. Religion was enclosed off by humanity. The twenty-first century demands that this expropriation of the divine by the human be undone. Human exceptionalism has become our fatal fetish, justifying limitless avarice and commodification as progress to freedom. Society must now be amended in service of a demos that surpasses the human, where nonhuman beings are ancient and indigenous citizens. Comrade metapersons must help us drown the sad freedom of possessive man.

The center of gravity of the political needs to be shifted from human beings to beings as such, from possessive men to communities. If state and capital both emphasize the sovereignty and self-contained individuality of their "I will," here we see a move away from "I will" to "I relate"—from individuality to relationality. But these declarations are still contained within the framework of the state. In Ecuador and Bolivia, as elsewhere on earth,

Indigenous movements and antiextractivist struggles have been repeatedly thwarted by state power. To unlock the full potential of these declarations, the settler-colonial-origin state needs to be dismantled, decolonization needs to be completed.

In his new book *The Climate of History in a Planetary Age*, Dipesh Chakrabarty argues that anticolonial Asian and African intellectuals and state builders were invested in exploiting the environment to achieve human prosperity: they shared with Europeans a fundamental belief in technological growth. He casts Jawaharlal Nehru, first prime minister of independent India, as a paradigmatic thinker here. For Chakrabarty, the goal of redistributive justice—stemming out of socialist, anti/postcolonial, and feminist discourses about subaltern well-being—seems oppositional to environmentalist concerns. The argument runs: if poor Indians, Chinese, and Africans demand the same living standards as Europeans and Americans—fuel-sucking air-conditioners and cars—it spells ecological disaster.

Our reading of anticolonial thought differs from Chakrabarty's. Nehruvian developmentalist ideology won only through tremendous violence—by suppressing popular revolutions in Telangana and Tripura; by submerging the antistatist thought of figures like Mahatma Gandhi and Kazi Nazrul Islam; by suppressing the decolonial antiextractivist environmentalism of Rabindranath Tagore; through settler-colonial operations, from northeast and central India to the Andamans and Kashmir. If strongman leadership and predatory capital conjoin today in India and other postcolonial states, the fatal bond has a prehistory. Similarly, Indian consumption aspirations today—air-conditioners to survive in a fossil fuel-heated world, cars to bypass an underfunded public transport system—cannot be understood without factoring in the prior violence of capital. In response to this capital-induced climate crisis, Dipesh Chakrabarty speaks of a "negative universal"—"a universal that arises from a shared sense of a catastrophe"—as the required thought for the Anthropocene. We urge political thought directly nourished by subaltern consciousness, that is, a new freedom struggle.

Modern liberal philosophy, which has colonized the Global North as well as elite consciousness in the Global South, assumes that we are discrete individuals. It assumes that we are (in C. B. Macpherson's words) "possessive individuals." The state exists to guarantee the anguish of our ownership rights. Recent advances in politics and science have rendered untenable the anthropocentric ground of liberalism.

Fungal Organization: Being inside Beings Is the Being within Me

In *Entangled Life*, the biologist Merlin Sheldrake urges us to recognize that beings do not exist in isolation. He draws his example from fungi, which exist in symbiosis with trees. Fungi exhibit communication abilities and problem-solving capacities—for example, finding the shortest route between two points—that often surpass those of humans. Contrary to literary images of the root as a singular ancestral entity—one nation, one root—in the real world, roots and fungi cling to each other, cooperating and nourishing together. Trees and fungi warn each other of enemies. Fungi also live together with algae and humans. Fungal networks store information as well as nutrients.

The *Chhandogya Upanishad* (seventh to sixth century BCE) relates how Aruni once asked his son Shvetaketu to fetch a fruit of the banyan tree. After Shvetaketu had cut open the fruit and then the seeds on his father's advice, Aruni instructed his son that the subtle essence that Shvetaketu could not see, from which the tree had grown, was the same essence that was the self of this whole world, the truth, the self. And this was also the essence of Shvetaketu. *Tat tvam asi*, that you are. In the light of Sheldrake's work, we can affirm: the essence that is within us humans, within trees, within fungi, exists in interdependence. We beings are a co-becoming. Being exists in the tiniest fungus, which itself exists in interdependence with other beings. We cannot see this subtle life-giving microscopic fungus, but it is what makes life possible. And this Being is also each of us. We are the fungus, we are the tree, we are Being. We are interdependence.

Sheldrake asks us to gaze deeper into our selves, to realize the fungi and other microorganisms that inhabit us, to recognize ourselves as ecosystems, to transform biology into ecology. What fungi are to the sciences, new Animism is to anthropology: it asks us to recognize the personhood of other-than-humans, even as we also vegetalize and animal-ize ourselves. As we peer into ourselves, as Shvetaketu did, we realize the Being that pervades us all. Aruni tells Shvetaketu that all beings have their root, resting place, foundation in *sat*, in Being. As we transform into Shvetaketu, we realize that without Being, nothing would exist—and this precisely is the interdependence of beings. Every being is Being and part of the interdependence, nourishing other beings. To become fungi is to walk the ladder of Being—to become angels ascending and descending to Being.

Fungal Democracy: Fungal Internationalism

In *Elementary Aspects of Peasant Insurgency*, Ranajit Guha recognized that territorial localism was both the strength and the weakness of subaltern resistance to capital and state. Confronted today by global capital, we cannot afford to take shelter in localized communities. Isolated communities are pulverized by state and capital, their internal hierarchies deepened by the inevitable penetration of capital, and they are exploited by states to co-opt their elites. To protect every subaltern community, to erode their internal inequalities of gender and class, these communities must work in cooperation. Subaltern Studies 2.0 studies these connections that are already being built and urges forging those yet to come.

Subaltern Studies 2.0 calls this the fungal organization. Against the great abstractions—nation, people, proletariat, universal class; against their antitheses—multiplicity, difference, incredulity; we propose Being as interdependence of beings, connection between beings, as unthinkable difference and nondifference (*a-chintya-bheda-abheda*), plurality of beings rooted in unity of Being. To become fungi is to recognize our responsibility to other beings: to restrain our desire, consumption, growth according to the needs of the many. To think like fungi is to abandon the Cartesian individualism that puts everything in doubt except the sovereign thinker. Against a human universe, we reclaim multibeing justice, a pluriverse. Happiness does not arise from the satisfaction of desire; it follows from duty to other beings.

Against the American Dream where every human being is a wealth-amassing individual, against British Prime Minister Margaret Thatcher's neoliberal slogan "There is no alternative," we say with the Zapatista revolutionaries of rural Mexico: let us create "a world where many worlds fit." *Un mundo donde quepan muchos mundos.* The fungal organization is this vast worlding between beings; it is what binds and bonds them together as *sakhas*, as *bandhus*. To be equal, *sama*, is to be together with, *saha*.

Against the Realpolitik definition of the political as resting on the distinction of friend and enemy, we call for an animist political that rests on the companionship of beings. Against Carl Schmitt, we invoke the Haudenosaunee Thanksgiving. The Native American Address publicly recognizes, acclaims, and thanks the people, earth, waters, fish, plants, animals, birds, winds, thunder, sun, moon, stars, teachers, and the creator. There was a religion before religion as sovereignty came into existence: an oblation of Being to Being. Its traces remain: in *pushpanjali*, the offering of flowers; in the divine speaking through sun, fire, and thunder. A trace also remains in the Haudenosaunee Thanksgiving—where the refrain of every oblation of gratitude is "now our minds are one."

In the last hymn of the *Rigveda*, the poet asks everyone to assemble and speak together, to agree together in their thoughts. The hymn insists that the utterance, the assembly, and the mind are all common, *samana*. The assembly, *samiti*, is where this commonness is achieved, where we are *samana*—a word that repeats itself across the prayer along with the prefix *sam-*, signifying "together." Deriving from the root *sam-*, much like the word *samaj*, the *samiti* is togetherness. The poet concludes, in this concluding verse of the *Rigveda*, that our hearts must be in common for our common purpose to be achieved.

There is a dense ground connection among being-together, *sam-*, being-equal, *sama*, and being-common, *samana*. This is the grammar of assembly—*samiti*; of community and society—*samaj*. All these terms are etymologically related, and are also cognates of English "same" and "similar"—rooted ultimately in Proto-Indo-European *sem. The *American Heritage Dictionary of Indo-European Roots*, edited by Calvert Watkins, defines *sem as "One; also adverbially 'as one,' together with." Here we witness an ancient grammar of oneness-togetherness of Being.

This togetherness of beings is what we must remember. Environmentalism was the first victim of the postcolonial state. Social justice came next. Today, we must unforget. We must regather the native oneness and equality that subaltern communities have never forgotten, and that nourished the anticolonial struggle. (There would be no Gandhi or Tagore without the forgotten Dalit-Bahujan-Adivasi villagers of India, whose consciousness—about nonviolence toward beings, about the commonness of the divine—they publicized.) At whatever level of power and influence we are, at whatever local or international scale we are operating at, we must recognize our common purpose today: the completion of decolonization through the eroding of state, the withering of capital.

Rooted Interdependence: Ancient Being, Return, Restore!

The apparatus that we propose is a fungal organization. In place of revolution, we urge involution; in place of party, we propose community; in place of an abstract universal class, we advocate ever-deepening solidarities between communities that already exist; in place of united nations, we propose united communities, a world fungus. To overcome the climate crisis, to scale down pollution-inducing extraction structures, to prevent the extinction of species, to erode the monstrous social inequality that exists, we need to harness concrete programs of degrowth and redistribution to a more fundamental rearrangement of life. We advocate for placing subaltern communities, human and other-than-human, at the center of all policy changes to regulate capital and pierce the veil of sovereign immunity claimed by states. Without this, top-down policy engineering is bound to fail, as the dismal record of the United Nations Framework Convention on Climate Change has clarified. Further, social justice, climate justice, demands that the rich must sacrifice and enjoy their sacrifice, and the material needs of the poor be simultaneously addressed. The rush for "net zero" carbon emissions, for degrowth, cannot proceed without the exacting scales of justice.

The light of Being gives beauty to all forms. Through our multiplicity, through our agreement, will emerge a democratic assembly, where the possessive individual—selfish private interest—shall wither away. The individual shall flourish through community—in relation with others. Individual and community are not each other's antitheses. Rather, both are true antitheses of state and capital that together stamp out idiosyncrasy, diversity—that yoke beings to the drudgery of exploitative labor. As the Indian poet and revolutionary Kazi Nazrul Islam observed, in accepting the government of others over ourselves, we become *sva-hin*, bereft of self, *nastika*, deniers of what is. In accepting the state, in living with capital, we lose ourselves, we deny Being.

Against the rootlessness of capital, against the fake root of the nation-state—majoritarian identity sugar-coating ruling-class exploitation—we uphold a rooted interdependence. As each works for the welfare of many, the exchange system of capital—each accumulating his own profit—will become obsolete. This in turn will render unnecessary and extraneous the state, the policeman of individual ownership, even before the state has been formally overthrown. The commodity form will steadily be replaced by the commons; commodification of beings will be whittled down. As feminists once called for wages for housework, we shall first demand wages for animals and plants who labor and create value for us. And then we shall replace the wage form altogether by an abundance where our communities will freely give what we require for being. Political education will replace advertising. Like Plato's horses, our desires will be reined in. Democratic collective planning shall be our charioteer. Humans will seek to understand animal polities with increased sensitivity and attune their decision making to the desires and welfare of animals. Scientific research will be directed toward establishing better communication between human and animal democracies. Humans will co-create vegetal polities with plants, with plant well-being code-termining public policy. Each being shall find their roots in another; each community shall work in solidarity with others. Each shall become a world for another. This is the restoration of Being. This is fungal organizational theory.

> One day these things will happen, and so even
>   now
> The sun rises, rain falls, and poems are written.
> —Nirendranath Chakravarti,
>   "Ekdin eisab habe, tai"

Beings in Assembly: Multibeing Demos

For millennia, humans have lived in society with animals and plants. Human polities have sometimes colonized animal polities and at other times kept a safe distance from them. Hence many, perhaps most, human societies have argued that laws should be addressed to human as well as nonhuman beings, governing their mutual relations.

In ancient India, the Code of Manu suggested that the distinction of law (*dharma*) and unlaw (*adharma*) held true not just for all humans but for all beings. As conservative Brahmanical texts, the law codes of Apastamba, Gautama, and Manu ranked animal species in relation to human caste order, prescribing different penalties for human killing of different animals. Buddhist texts were generally less crudely hierarchical. The Buddha proclaimed *dharma/dhamma* for the happiness of all beings. The *Lalitavistara* observes that the wheel of law (*dharmachakra*) follows the voices/cries of all beings (*sarvasattvarutacharanam*); the word *ruta* is often used for animal utterances. Buddhist lawgivers like Padmasambhava addressed human as well as nonhuman beings.

In early modern eastern India, the Chandimangal tradition described a multispecies demos, where forest animals and lower-caste humans were heroes, high-caste humans villains. The tradition prescribed norms restricting conflict (*avirodha*) between species. In the

Sundarbans, Muslims and Hindus venerate the tiger god Dakshin Ray, the Muslim saint Bara Khan Ghazi, and the semi-Muslim Bonbibi, Forest Lady. A pact of friendship (in late seventeenth- and early eighteenth-century *Raymangal* texts: *dostani*, *maitra*) was sealed between Dakshin Ray and the Muslim powers to share authority over this mangrove forest delta. This enabled an ethos of human-tiger coexistence that still shapes the region. Similarly, medieval Christian texts mention saints living close to animals and instituting peace between different species. A fourteenth-century Italian hagiography noted how Francis of Assisi concluded a peace pact (*il patto della pace*) between a wolf and the assembled people of the Italian town of Gubbio, prohibiting mutual killing and ensuring that the citizens fed the wolf daily.

Multispecies norm frameworks were often traditionally articulated through oral, visual, and performative communication, rather than through writing. In Aboriginal Australia, the Dreaming regulates conduct between human and nonhuman beings; it is now recognized as Indigenous customary law. In many societies there have been either prohibitions or, more frequently, ritually controlled restrictions on hunting. Indiscriminate hunting, especially of mating, pregnant, and young animals, has often been discouraged. We find such rules circumscribing hunting of tapir among the Yanomami in the Amazon, of polar bear among the Arctic Inuit, and of the tiger among the Naga.

Across the past few centuries, colonial state and capital have conspired to exile nonhumans from the multispecies polities that had existed in many parts of the premodern world. This great expulsion is the precondition for modern states and constitutions. Human law is omnipotent in modern single-species legislatures. If nonhumans are sometimes protected, it is only through the capricious benevolence of a legal system that essentially serves capital. Hence today, we must recall ancient and living multispecies polities—we must reinvigorate diverse vocabularies of interspecies pact making—in order to construct a more-than-human planetary demos. However, we cannot merely reproduce the old ways—we must overcome class, gender, ethnic/caste, and species inequalities.

This shall be a cosmic constitution. Unlike state constitutions, it shall not be a fixed document. The will of the people shall be overthrown. Humans shall learn to restrain their will to enable the weal and happiness of all beings. Like the Buddhist wheel of law, this law must rotate—continually transform in response to the hopes and fears of all beings, negating every axis of domination. Law will vary across space and time, perpetually self-reforming through conversations and friendship pacts between human and nonhuman assemblies.

The Vanquishing of Unbeing

Here is Kailasa
Farther north of the Himalaya
Called by those who know
Axis and measuring rod of the Earth.
Here in her home the Earth
Upholder of all beings
Put possessive man to trial
For crimes against Being.
She summoned all beings
To bear witness against man.

When they had indicted man
She spoke:
Possessive man
Binding the world in a net
Traps himself in that net.
He sees his own self in what he owns
Makes property his proper self.
In possessing others
He possesses himself.

A voice roared:
I, Swe, primal possessor
Rule all beings as state
Devour all beings as capital.
I dismember Being
Allot who would be master

Who slave.
Who the head
Who the foot.

Awake beings
Awake lions
Awake cave-hiding dawn
Throw off your commodity funeral shrouds.

I have seen a god in mortal form
Eyes of fire, burning ember
An angel in yoke that pierced my heart
And my voice can be silent no more.

Mountains, rivers, animals, and plants spoke in chorus:
We are gods
Luminous beings
Toward whom humans have irrevocable obligations.
Truth
Steadfast and firm-footed
Whose form is friendship
Binds us in community.

The greater a being's power
The more intense its duty to others.
God is the coming into presence of Being
That connects us all as fellow beings.
Divinity is that which is common to us all
The third that makes two one.

Being had been lost, had been hidden, had been forgotten
It had passed to the other shore.
This great negation is now negated.
Being recollects itself.
Being is light forgotten and remembered
The separation of mine and yours annulled.

All beings dismembered Swe—
Your form is unreal
Emptiness is your form.
When men thirst for profit and power
You become their dream
And hang like a nightmare over others.
Insubstantial monster conjured by desire.

The state does not give us liberty
Money does not make us free.

The holy assembly
Set this monster to fire
Sacrificing Unbeing to Being.

They swore an unwavering oath.
The age of artificial persons
Was over.
Being revealed itself in fullness
In the luminous forms of all beings.

Beings Turn the Wheel of Law

We, the beings of the Earth
Having sacrificed possessive man to all beings,
Immolating Unbeing to Being,
With common mind,
Move the Wheel of Law,
To abolish the state, to scatter away capital,
For the well-being of the many
For the happiness of the many.
Gathered in assemblies
Multibeing demos
The Wheel of Law pursues different paths
Fullness to fullness, in fullness of speech,
Different norms in different assemblies,
Deliberating in different languages,
But always following the cries of all beings.
To reduce harm to beings,
Never to be subject to another,
Never to exploit another,
Through compassion, generosity, self-restraint,
Regarding every self as myself,
Be each other's friend, truth bound in interdependence.
Earth is our witness.

The Constitution of the Cosmos

Turn I: Rekin

From the Himalayan ranges to the Tibetan Plateau and beyond, every being is kin of another. The Bhutanese say *semchen tham chen pha-ma een*, all sentient beings are parents of one another. Kinship extends beyond the biotic. *Gnas ri-s*, abode mountains, are sibling deities. Himalaya has the soul of a god—father alike of Ganga, the river that sustains the plains, and of Parvati, Mountain Lady, revered in India as universal mother. As Haimavati, Daughter of the Snow-Clad, Parvati is visible in the very first moment of Indian philosophy: revealing Being to humble the gods. Here, glaciers become confluences of heaven and earth. Lakes in the Plateau channel life spirit and oracles. Farther, more ranges, the Hindu Kush, the Pamir Mountains—Meru, *sakha*, companion, of Himalaya.

As one ascends into the mountains, the air thickens with divinities. Being unconceals as *termas*, treasure texts, that mountains, cliffs, and lakes regularly reveal to humans. Parvati and her husband, Shiva, dwell at Kailasa, by the Mind Lake, Manasa Sarovara, united as speech and meaning, *vagarthaviva*. Padmasambhava, Gesar, and other more-than-humans deliberate here about *chos*. These norms are renewed in storytelling, verse, geomancy, augury—in an ethnographic and folkloric epic constituted by inseparable speech between beings. Industrialization, mining, construction require the permission of the land's divine guardians. Local norms sometimes reiterate the authority of traditional elites and sometimes support subaltern resistance against elites. The Tibetan Epic of Gesar urges overthrowing "those who feed on the substance of beings and spread suffering."

Three nuclear leviathans have partitioned this norm world today. The Chinese state pulverizes Buddhists in Tibet and Uyghur Muslims in Xinjiang. Hindu nationalist India subdues Muslims in Kashmir and Ladakh and Christians in highland northeast India. Pakistani juntas smash diverse minorities.

Padmasambhava commands: "Protect the beings that the demons wish to afflict, remove their sufferings and let them all rejoice in your exploits."

State partners with capital in the roof of the world. Deforestation, mining, hydroelectric power projects, military highways, uncontrolled industrialization, urbanization, irrigation, demographic re-engineering, periodic warfare—these disintegrate millennia-old ecosystems. Carbon emissions hasten retreat of glaciers, imperiling river systems that feed billions of humans and many more nonhumans across South and East Asia.

Gesar prays: "That among men, some be not mighty and others deprived of power; that some abound not in riches whilst others lack them; that all beings be happy!"

In the Andes, *tirakuna*, earth beings, have joined with *runakuna*, human beings; in Aotearoa, Te Awa Tupua, Te Urewera, and Mount Taranaki have assembled with Maori peoples; Native Hawaiians have assembled with Mauna Kea; Niyamgiri, Law Mountain, stands with his Dongria Kondh offspring. Mountains and their human kin have assembled in revolution today.

Gesar counsels: "Abstain from all traffic, envy, and greediness. Desire the welfare of all beings, work for it in an effective manner."

Assemblies turn the wheel of law.

The first principle—nonkilling. State shall not colonize community.

The second principle—nonstealing. Capital shall not prey on beings.

Imperial state shall wither away before native multibeing assemblies.

Human citizenship shall be replaced by kinship of all beings.

Human law overwritten by multibeing norms.

Constraining industrialization, mining, construction—mandatory permission from the land's protectors, human and more-than-human.

Reining in production and consumption—the consent and happiness of beings.

A prayer of benediction resounds from the Gangetic Plains to the Tibetan Plateau: "May the rain fall in time, and the earth abound with crops, may beings flourish."

From the highlands has awakened a cosmic constitution with many names: the rights of the Earth in South America, the indivisible personhood of mountain, river, and human in New Zealand. A refusal to be subject, a denial to be commodity, a negation of the separation of biotic and abiotic—a constitution for all beings.

Being is interdependence—one not two.

Turn II: Renomad

The nomad's home is Being.

Every year, multitudes of birds spend the winter in the South Asian plains, and return to Highland Asia for summer. Indian humans, late arrivals to the region compared to wild geese, may well have learned from the older denizens about some of the passes to cross the Himalayan ranges. (It is believed that ancient Polynesian mariners discovered the Hawaiian Islands by following migrating birds.)

Kalidasa's fifth-century epic *Meghaduta* represents a broader Sanskrit tradition when it suggests that to traverse the Himalayas to Tibet, one should go through the crane pass, *krauncharandhra*, the gateway of the geese, *hamsadvara*. In Abanindranath Tagore's novel *Buro Angla* (1920-21), the geese guide a boy from Bengal to the Himalaya. The Swedish explorer Sven Hedin tracked wild geese while traveling from India to Tibet, observing that the intelligent birds lived in tribes, collectively transmitting cartographic knowledge about migration routes to future generations. Their in-flight quacks were tribal deliberations.

Countless verses welcome migrating birds to India in autumn. Rabindranath Tagore sang about ruddy shelducks (Bengali, *chakha chakhi*):

> The bee forgets to drink honey today,
> Drunk in light, it flies around,
> With what aim do the *chakha chakhi*
> Gather in river islands today.

In India, the *hamsa*—the goose and the rarer swan—has long symbolized the soul. Its flight epitomizes the soul's return to the divine. By association, Tibet, where geese return to breed in summer, acquired a divine aura. Indians connected the *hamsa* especially with one Tibetan lake, naming it Manasa Sarovara, Lake of Consciousness. The *Mahabharata* calls Manasa *satyatoya*, whose water is truth. Socrates compared the dying philosopher to the dying swan returning to Apollo, god of wisdom. To Indians, the noble *hamsa* embodied the nostos to Being, homecoming to consciousness.

Across millennia, pilgrims, merchants, herders, scholars traveled between Tibet and India. Today, hostile states have finally closed the border.

Let us free land animals from this imprisonment by the state—reanimalize the map.

Avianize territory—no state borders, and self-restraint on interbeing conflict.

Species have long migrated and coexisted without mutual extermination. There are territorial conflicts among migrating birds, but no human-type imperial conquests and genocides. Hence they inspire anarchist political theory.

> Take, for instance, one of the numberless
> lakes of the Russian and Siberian Steppes. Its
> shores are peopled with myriads of aquatic
> birds, belonging to at least a score of different
> species, all living in perfect peace—all protecting one another.
>
> —Peter Kropotkin,
> *Mutual Aid: A Factor of Evolution*

Humans destabilized frameworks of shared living—for example, by selectively breeding domestic animals to massively increase their sexual productivity, and removing spaces where wild animals thrive. State borders reduce multibeing assemblies to demarcated territories, where each state has sovereign impunity to harm beings to extract labor and resources.

In Bhutan, humans have of late been introducing dogs and horses into the highlands at an accelerated rate. Yaks not only are forbidden access to Tibet but also must compete with horses for limited grasslands—humans see horses as less recalcitrant laborers. Herders complain that dog feces lower grass quality and damage yak physical and mental health.

State—closure of borders—and capital—selective breeding in the longue durée—co-create this crisis.

State borders—which enable capital to circulate, while the poor perish; which ghettoize free animals—shall be abolished.

In the multibeing demos, norms and decisions about migration shall be informed by the weal and happiness of the multitudes. Continual conversations between human and nonhuman assemblies shall guide decisions. Human and nonhuman polities shall again move freely, while caring for each other's well-being—an ancient multispecies nomadism revived.

Beings shall pasture freely. Nomadism is the original nomos.

The Bhutanese welcome crane collectives, who annually migrate from Tibet to South Asia, with song and dance; ensure their welfare and penalize violence against them; pray for their safe migration back in spring; venerate them as wisdom-beings.

Poor humans die at Fortress Europe's Mediterranean border; are incarcerated when they enter the United States; are persecuted when they travel for livelihood from Bangladesh to India.

Let states not police the movements of the destitute and the hungry. Let prosperous societies welcome and venerate those who seek shelter.

Through nomadism—the nostos.

Through joyful hospitality to the subaltern—return to Being.

Turn III: Reanimate

Grass is the foundation of Being.

For millennia, herbivores have fed on grass. Omnivores, including humans, as well as carnivores feed in turn on herbivores. Across ancient Eurasia, pastoralist humans followed cattle and horses, who in turn followed the grass. As humans moved, so did their gods—but always they came and sat on the grass.

> Listen, you with listening ears, along with
>   your passengers,
> The gods who travel with you, o Agni.
> Let them sit on the ritual grass—
> Mitra, Aryaman, and those who travel early to
>   the ceremony.
> —*Rigveda*, tr. Stephanie Jamison

Humans would associate and compare their gods with cattle and horses; the mobile animals in turn got a share of divinity. A hymn thus addresses divine Fire as a horse:

> Spur forth now Jatavedas, the prizewinning
>   horse,
> To sit here on this ritual grass of ours.
> —*Rigveda*, tr. Stephanie Jamison

Virgil recounts in the *Aeneid* how ancient Italians built grassy altars—*arae gramineae*—for the gods. In India, until today, the gods are invited to sit down for a meal and a drink, welcomed especially with *durva* grass.

The *Lalitavistara* embodies a wider Buddhist tradition when it describes how the Buddha realized that the seat where he would attain enlightenment had to be a grass seat (*trinasamstara*)—following the ancient custom of previous beings who had thus achieved awakening. In Bhutan, people visualize the Buddhist *om mani padme hum* mantra manifesting in the grass. Grass, as foundation of Being, is logos—enlightenment, a return to the freedom of the steppes.

> Because you would become blessed,
> Feeding upon good pasturage,
> So then we would also be blessed.
> Feed on grass always, o inviolable cow [=Speech]!
> Coming here, drink pure water!
> —*Rigveda*, tr. Joel Brereton

For millennia, humans have recognized the personhood of grass. The *Rigveda* sings: "O divine Ritual Grass, with a mind without anger sacrifice to the gods." Among Native Americans, sweetgrass is Mother Earth's fragrant hair.

A few millennia ago, humans began domesticating select grass types to produce cereals.

For many communities, an agricultural field is a multibeing demos, where the interdependence between beings is nurtured through care and self-restraint.

Swidden cultivation embodies this demos. In the Naga hills, *jhum* fields involve camaraderie between humans, fungi, soil-exhausting crops like rice, soil-enriching crops like legumes, chilies, tubers, and solanums. Plants, fungi, and soil exchange fluids, nutrients, and intelligence. They buffer and shelter each other from insects, pests, and droughts. Postharvest, the land is idled and entreated to recuperate.

Modern scholarship calls this biodiversity. Like many other swidden cultivators, the Nagas personify the beings involved in this collaboration as spirits. Farmers nourish the spirits of sky and earth with offerings. The Nagas chant, "O terhuomia, be gracious, let there be many blossoms this year." They ask forgiveness from the spirits of animals killed by the burning of the slash. They sing to earth and plants, "Today we come to clean you. Grow well and bear good fruits." They follow bird song and behavior to learn about weather and diseases.

Rituals and prohibitions guard every step of cultivation, from forest slashing to seed sowing to weed cleaning to harvesting. Those involved in cultivation are persons, not commodities—cultivation is reciprocity between animate beings. Their being remains tenacious even today, despite the spread of Christianity among the Nagas across the early-to-mid-twentieth century. God may reign in heaven, but the spirits continue to influence the fields.

Animism is the abstraction of the intersubjective *jhum* field, as it is of the grassland.

Animism is the theology of the nomadic multibeing demos.

As coercive labor and resource extraction developed in many human societies, class differences and antagonisms crystallized. The state emerged to protect property and guarantee inequality. Rulers found swidden agriculture difficult to tax, and capital accumulators found it difficult to extract monetary value from. Hence they generally encouraged a shift to sedentary agriculture, a transition that was often easier to implement in the plains than in the highlands. As social hierarchy intensified, the labor and ritual of multispecies social reproduction was increasingly relegated to women and subaltern classes.

In the alluvial Bengal plains, agrarian *brata* rituals are therefore often performed by women. The multispecies demos remains tenacious, though subordinated to state power, class/caste hierarchy, and patriarchy. Women recognize as persons the Earth, trees, rain and river water, cattle—collaboration among these beings enables life. Plants grow here not in monoculture isolation, but in relation with other beings. Women draw *alpana* diagrams on soil to visualize these multibeing intimacies.

> The banyan is here, the white fig is here, the
>   basil is in her abode,
> I perform the earth ritual in the midst of three
>   trees.
> Flower in mother's lineage, fruit in father's
>   lineage, star in father-in-law's lineage,

The stream of Ganga water shall descend to
  the three lineages.
The earth will float in water.
    —Basudhara Brata—Abanindranath Tagore,
                     Banglar Brata

Human women clean bovine women with water, anoint their horns with oil, decorate their foreheads with turmeric, vermilion, and sandalwood paste, comb their head, and hold a mirror before them. Human women offer bovine women *durva* grass and bananas, fan them, and sing:

Cow grass (*gokal*) living in the cow herd sacred
  land (*gokul*),
By giving grass to the cow's mouth,
Let me live in paradise.
             —Gokul Brata–Ashutosh Majumdar,
                   Meyeder Brata-Katha

In Bengali homes, women perform most household labor. They look after Bastulakshmi, goddess of the household foundation. In the example best known to us, Bastulakshmi is venerated in the form of an earthen pot with soil, rice grains, cowrie shells, a conch shell, coins, and a *rudraksha* seed. Betel leaf and areca nut are also sometimes associated. (The agrarian field links here with maritime trade, source of cowrie currency and conch.) The Bastulakshmis of the different households are annually reunited with the lineage deity, embodying the interdependence of the broader kin group.

The *brata* is the poetry of the multibeing demos; *alpana*, its diagram; Bastulakshmi, its icon. This demos—which has been subjugated by human patriarchy, yoked to the service of possessive man—needs immediate liberation.

Modern capitalism is impatient about such delicate interdependence among beings that shapes traditional swidden as well as settled agriculture. It seeks to accelerate the pace of labor and resource extraction, of profit and capital accumulation.

Jhum multicropping on moving fields disperses crops and confounds easy fiscal assessment and appropriation. Therefore, across northeast India, the British sought to substitute it with plantation agriculture, especially of tea.

Plantation agriculture is multispecies slavery.

It historically involved slave labor—as in Caribbean sugar plantations and American cotton plantations—as well as semiservile labor—as in the tea plantations of India. Humans were reduced to the extreme abjection of the commodity form. Even today, plantations across the world subsist on human unfreedom.

Capitalist agriculture also enslaves plants. Plant well-being is often compromised—deformed and diseased plants bred—to ensure profit maximization. There is reduced scope for multispecies plant communication and plant intelligence. Pesticides are toxic to human and nonhuman species. Soil and water are contaminated. There is radical depletion of biodiversity, with monoculture eradicating complex millennia-old ecosystems. Corporate control of agriculture engenders peasant impoverishment and compromises food security, especially for subaltern populations in the Global South. Humans grow addicted to tea, coffee, sugar, cocoa, and similar products. As humanity enslaves plants, plants also enslave humans. Capital, ultimate slave master, harnesses multiple species in its expansion.

The British were not entirely successful in northeast India. Nagas and other Indigenous peoples resisted plantation agriculture. They resisted being transformed into wage slaves, their fields turned into factories.

Inspired by Indigenous rebellion, we demand the liberation of the field.

*Jhum*ming guarantees biodiversity—it shapes the earth as multibeing life. Surviving Zomia communities, who sustained nomadic agriculture across millennia, never taking more than ecosystems could regenerate, shall illumine our way. We shall re-*jhum* the world.

Swidden agriculture flourished until state and capital overran *jhum* communities and forbade them to let land remain fallow. State and capital encouraged unsustainable population growth of humans and of domestic animals and plants, in order to extract cheap labor and resources, expand tax bases and markets, and maximize profits. Nonstate humans and nondomestic animals and forests were labeled as wild—treated as vermin—exterminated or subjugated.

We shall remember and globalize the animist social contract.

Across swidden fields of South and Southeast Asia, humans regularly negotiate social contracts with other humans, with other-than-human beings, with Earth. These contracts embody promises and permissions. They are the living constitution of the more-than-human demos.

The Garo peoples of the northeast Indian highlands annually renew their social contract with land god Saljong. The god gifts them rice grains; Garos offer him in return cooked rice, fish, rice beer, and the smoke of burning pine resin (*sasat*). The Garo creation epic—*dani*—is recounted to seal this contract.

A Garo elder chants:

> Saljong:
> To the father of millet
> To the good Saljong
> For all the months of the year
> For all seasons
> Making a promise
> Sworn at the smoke
> Till the cotton tree buds like charcoal
> Till the *mandal* tree blooms
> Making a promise
> Sworn at the smoke
> Saljong.
>   (Recorded and translated by Erik de Maaker)

Garos negotiate an annual social contract with Minima, the mother of rice. She guarantees the good harvest—humans acknowledge that they have to kill her but emphasize that they shall uphold harmony in togetherness with plants and gods.

> The neck of the rice stalk has been hacked (...)
> The mother of rice has been killed (...)
> Plants, come out, and grow in any direction.
> Be in harmony with each other, and with the spirits.
> (Recorded and translated by Erik de Maaker)

Naga farmers traditionally make social contracts with spirits and other beings. These involve propitiation and offerings as well as challenges, defiance, even occasional threats. A Naga *Kümvo*, intercessor of spirits, might say before clearing a fresh patch of earth:

> We intend to uphold the peace between humans and all spirits living here.
> To the spirits of the streams, the stones, and the jungle, we say:
> Let there be no rivalry between us.
> Let there be no destruction and death. Let us collaborate.
> You are honest. We are honest.
> Let us be honest.

Across South and Southeast Asia, speakers of Tibeto-Burman and Austroasiatic languages create these social contracts. Their historical migrations across Asia spread cultivation, including of rice, and their distinctive ways of forging the more-than-human demos. Many of these communities have continued to practise swidden cultivation until modern times.

Yet historians and philosophers have scarcely paid any attention to them. They remain obsessed with the birth of states—Mesopotamia, Egypt, Persia, Rome—neglecting equally ancient nonstate civilizations encompassing vast nomadic geographies that remain alive today. This has consequences for political theory.

In the Western canon of political theory, the social contract is forged once—the people, having assembled, give birth to the state and abdicate to it their powers. The people may retain a right to resist and revolt, but this is not meant to be a regular occurrence.

The animist social contract makes humans responsible not just to other humans but also to nonhuman beings—to spirits of cereals, animals, waters, forests. As swidden communities move across land, they continually negotiate new social contracts with new neighbors. Hence, the animist contract is not a one-time affair that founds the state—its regular rites keep reshaping multibeing demos. It is nomadic constitutionalism.

In the Christian social contract—Locke is emblematic—the creator God gives Adam and his descendants unlimited powers to subdue and possess the earth. The animist social contract denies humans such powers.

The modern revolution descends from European traditions of social contract theory and popular resistance. Humans wage revolution to liberate other humans. An apocalyptic battle transfigures the political system.

We call for animist revolution. This is not one-time Armageddon—it is patient and perennial negotiations between beings, for the joy of many species.

The Christian God's creation is the blueprint for the modern revolutionary's dream to build a new world. Christian paradise, secularized, is revolutionary utopia. Animist revolution refuses utopia—the hell of eternal perfection. It moves in flux with the wheel of life.

The Communist Revolution's tragedy was that it arose and was globalized through ancient state societies like Russia and China. Hence, revolution became a state-creating commandment, not a state-destroying struggle. Lenin, Stalin, and Mao became new Gods and Caesars. Socialism degenerated into state capitalism.

Global revolution shall look different if it awakens from nonstate communities.

Animisms have been hitherto exterminated, as by Christian imperialism, or shackled, as by Brahmanical caste. The new revolution shall be the eruption of subjugated Animisms.

Against the constituent moment, the one-time revolutionary founding—an eternal revolution.

Animism is rooted nomadism.

Animist cultivation is multispecies flourishing. Animist recognition of nonhuman sentience shall partner with scientific research about plant and animal intelligence to foster biodiverse farming. Animist revolutionaries shall also work with other precapitalist, preplantation, premonoculture forms of indigenous agriculture to ensure multispecies food security. Where precapitalist traditions no longer exist, new rewilding will be nurtured. State societies shall restrain the growth of their populations—of humans and domestic plants and animals—in order to allow nonstate humans, nondomestic plants and animals, space to flourish.

Communities shall protect biodiversity. Simultaneously, they shall be reformed. Women and other subalterns shall not shoulder disproportionate responsibility for multispecies social reproduction. Gender justice, class justice, and species justice shall converge. Specific decisions shall be taken through constant conversations between human and nonhuman polities.

Plants and animals shall be freed from monoculture isolation. As they are unshackled, humans shall be unshackled from corporate control over labor force, markets, and governments. Humans shall vegetalize.

> Be humbler than the grass, be tolerant as the
> tree,
> Not concerning yourself with honor, give
> honor to others.
>
> —Chaitanya, "Shikshashtakam"

Social contract is the original literature. The most ancient poetry, the most living poetry, is what forges interdependence between beings, what lays down norms of mutual harmony, like the Garo and Naga chants. From this interdependence arise the figures of speech, the ornaments of language, the meters of prosody. Contemporary literature, in turning away from the nonhuman, has ceased to ally with revolution—it merely punctuates bourgeois work.

To return to Animism is to make literature possible once more as the connection of human and other-than-human—to repoeticize the world. The poetry of the future rises from the past.

Against Adam—we invoke the gods of grass and grain.

Against individual property—collective nourishing.

Against profit—multispecies well-being.

Against accumulation and growth—self-restraint and degrowth.

Against abstract value—pan-being sustainable intelligence.

Against commodities—we invite the spirits of forest and field.

Turn IV: Rewild

Kabir the weaver sings:

> Listen sage, the Brahmin priest is a clever butcher.
> Slaughtering a goat, he chases the sheep—
> No mercy comes to his heart.
> And then he says to the assembly—
> How holy he is,
> Such a high lineage.

In the highlands of Bhutan persists one of the world's oldest forms of colonialism, as well as one of the longest-running anticolonial rebellions. Humans have enslaved the yak polity by exiling its leader, the *zholu*, substituting the human herdsman and castrating the remaining males. Yet, revolt continues. When herders pile too heavy a load on the backs of male yaks, and whenever they try to milk the women too forcefully, the yaks retaliate with hard kicks, head butts, wild galloping, slamming their horns on the ground in rage, and/or complete refusal to move. In response, herders tie their legs and beat their backs with sticks.

From time to time, the contagion of revolt spreads widely. Some yaks emit a special grunt to communicate with other yaks and disseminate insubordination. Often, yaks organize into a collective hard gaze, directed toward cruel herders. (A similar gaze is directed at unfamiliar humans who get too close to them without their consent.) As resistance spreads, the herdsmen retaliate like any colonial power—by isolating, punishing, and when necessary, killing the yak rebel vanguard, to browbeat the herd into submission.

The master-slave dialectic, contra Hegel, is not confined to humanity. The slave's autonomous consciousness, developed in resistance to the master's command, manifests through gestures and grunts.

As in other premodern polities, there is space for benevolence. Sensitive colonizers, especially from subaltern classes, translate the grief of the colonized. The Bhutanese herdsman poet Ap Chuni Dorji thus assumes the yak's person in a popular song:

> I am enjoying my stay in this peaceful meadow, but I can see a place where my kind is slaughtered in the distance.
>
> Even though the place where I am staying is peaceful, I cannot help but be sad when I see the slaughterhouse.
>
> Because of karma, I must experience the same sadness and fate at the end. I cannot help but accept my destiny.
>
> When a powerful lord commands, someone will come with a sword to end my life.
>
> It is time for me to go, because they have come to take me. I have no choice but to follow them.

Modern research confirms the stress animals experience on the way to slaughterhouses. Occasionally, they try to escape.

The lord, *rgyal*, stands condemned. How shall this master-yak dialectic become a revolution?

The yak polity must be decolonized.

The *zholu* shall be allowed to rejoin the herd. The herdsman's monarchic power over the herd shall be checked by the yak monarch.

Male yaks shall no more be castrated. As they compete for power and prestige with the *zholu*, monarchy will be replaced by polycracy.

No more forced impregnation of yaks by the *zholu*. After centuries, yak women will freely select their lovers and decide for themselves if and when to get pregnant.

Wherever possible, humans shall encourage yaks to revolt. Human feminists may work with yak women to ensure a gender-egalitarian yak revolution. Existing female resistance, especially to milking, may intensify into a post-colonial yak feminism.

Until a few decades ago, yaks could travel across the Himalayas and the Tibetan Plateau, freely choosing their pastures. As herder societies followed yak societies, nomadic human territorialities crystallized around nomadic yak territorialities. Following China's conquest of Tibet, a well-patrolled border has emerged between Tibet and Bhutan. Conversations with old herders suggest that the yaks were initially bewildered when they were stopped from traveling to their old pastures. Even now, herders occasionally use force to prevent yaks from crossing the border. With less pasture available, overgrazing lowers yak standards of living.

Yaks shall graze freely.

As yak polities cross borders, freedom of movement must also be restored to their human herdsmen turned comrades.

Yaks shall vanguard the overthrow of state borders.

Bhutanese cattle colonialism allows sensitivity toward animals. Ancient norms limit mistreatment of cattle. Kinship ties humans and cattle in asymmetrical bonds of care. Slaughterhouses are rare. The Western-modern animal industry exterminates young male cattle and poultry deemed unproductive, while productive animals are allowed to grow up to be slaughtered. No traditional norms constrain killing for profit. Animal rights laws and lax meat inspection systems are inadequate before the industrial scale of murder. Despite laws about stunning, animals are often dismembered, scalded, and flayed alive. Forced impregnation of female animals in intensive live-stock farming leads to widespread injury and mortality of mothers and infants.

Twentieth-century states have perpetrated genocide against humans on a scale that premodern states never envisaged. Similarly, against the animal world, modern state and capital are waging a genocidal war without any precedent. State-capital is a Janus-faced machine of mass castration, mass rape, mass extermination. Greenhouse gas emissions engendered by the meat industry accelerate global warming.

Subaltern humans—such as low-paid lower-caste laborers in India and nonwhite laborers in the United States—bear the physical and psychological stress of the industry, while profits accrue to the rich. In India, Muslim/lower-caste animal handlers confront social discrimination and are occasionally lynched by Hindu-chauvinist mobs.

The capitalist meat industry is multispecies colonialism. It must be criminalized. It must be abolished.

> It is a heavy crime to kill creatures.
> The pitiless do not understand the pain felt by
>   living beings;
> They kill living beings for a taste.
> Kabir says—Look at Being!
> God shines in all creatures.

Animal husbandry must return to preindustrial forms, such as practiced in Bhutan and other similar societies in the Global South, as preparation for a more comprehensive animal revolution. Radical economic boycotts of the meat industry will be essential. Further, mass civil disobedience techniques of the kind that brought down the British Empire in India shall be deployed to dismantle meat capitalism.

Human workers shall be offered alternative employment.

Animal liberation shall be carried out in camaraderie with subaltern actors—like Dalit-Bahujans in India—who have traditionally looked after nonhuman beings: in whose poetry and music, animals shine more than in the archives of elites.

Modern scientific research shows that domestication significantly reduced brain size among animals. For example, the brain size of dogs is about one-third less than that of gray wolves, with a similar reduction in pigs, compared to wild boars. Over twelve millennia, humans engineered artificial selection to ensure that animals would resist them less—in human parlance, show less aggression or wariness. Today, humans must help strengthen animal resistance to human power—help animal senses and cerebral capacities flourish.

We do not expect humans to entirely abandon animal products. But they shall prioritize animal happiness over profit and overindulgence in animal products. For example, humans may milk cattle while ensuring that calves have adequate milk and remain with their mothers. They must offer cattle delicious and nutritious food, comfortable habitation, beautiful pastures, and many vacations. They may entertain cattle with music—scientific reportage suggests that cows appreciate music.

Forced impregnation and carceral life shall be replaced by free love and family.

No more an atomized proletariat living for death—animals shall live in free collectives, as political beings.

The ways to achieve this shall vary between the industrial world, where domestic animals have been overwhelmingly proletarianized, and the preindustrial world, where there remain spaces of subaltern-nonhuman autonomy.

Specific details of reciprocity shall be worked out through continuous conversations between human and animal polities. Traditional human knowledge, especially subaltern peasant-pastoral knowledge, about animal consciousness—distinction between sounds, gestures, and gaze of happiness and affection, and those of pain and revolt—will dialogue with scientific scholarship. Humans shall do all to ascertain what keeps animals happy—an egalitarian return to human-animal kinship.

Animals are beings, not commodities. They shall be fellow citizens and comrades, not slaves.

Being Triumphant

Capital transforms beings into commodities. Capital is Unbeing.

    Beings of the World Unite!

    To escape general extinction
    Universal death
    Root yourself in Being
    Realize the interdependence of beings!

    Know Being! There is no other path!

Exhortations

The Next Steps

A Preface

Gayatri Chakravorty Spivak

Literature gives you the experience of the impossible. Christine Brooke-Rose's *Subscript* allowed me to say, at the conference on diversity in the sociology department of the elite Islamic university in Delhi, Jamia Milia Islamia:

> Let us begin with "Being," philosophy thinking the human, the human as animal, as part of an animal world living in biodiversity leading upstream from the human, to the very first cell which by chance emerges out of the pre-biotic soup. This is the contemporary charge for thinking this word in English. I bypass the awesome obligation to think of how the world's wealth of languages would think or not think this word. Plural epistemologies indeed. Different ways of knowing. The mother as honor, the daughter as reproductive right, and then in all the languages of the world.

But, I reminded myself, to say it is not to have established that desire as an ethical reflex in either myself or the many human beings I come in contact with every day, because I am a paid humanities teacher. I believe the authors of this pamphlet, Milinda Banerjee and Jelle Wouters, are aware of this, and of the tremendous task ahead of them. To say it is not to have done it.

Confronted with the fact that the Metropolitan Museum of New York has made a land acknowledgment to the First Nations of this area, I was obliged to close my keynote to the Asia Society of New York on the topic of "Reimagining Museum Narratives in the Twenty-First Century" in this way:

> We should all learn to undo our minds to realize that (ourselves as) the world itself—and this is everyone—can only acknowledge that it was imposed on commons. For this, one of our tasks (indicated by suggestions, for example, to the World Economic Forum and Comparative Education Society) is to impart to the subaltern indigenous a real sense of the cartographic world, rather than dwell on the fact that most indigenous languages have a word for "world," but not for "colonialism" or "deconstruction." How is this tremendous epistemological performance, sustained by imaginative activism rather than cost-effectiveness, to be achieved? Perhaps it will hit us by creative chance (Aristotle calls this tuchè) as we perform the short-term tasks assiduously, without personal politics; or, bigger

yet, let us turn to the end of that citation from the mad mathematician/philosopher Ludwig Wittgenstein: "when we arbitrarily conceptualize something ... we are not surprised by those pictures enough to say, 'Look there!'" (trans. modified). We must wait for the reimagined meta-museality as dictated by the planetary to surprise us.[1]

Elsewhere I have suggested that thoroughly decentralized worldwide groups practice teacher training on these principles, listening to the subaltern rather than simply romanticizing it or judging it premodern, prepolitical. But the work of making the cartographic map heartfelt for the subaltern is essential. I have been engaged in this for some time, with a deep and local focus, but for people who cannot travel at all, it is not easy to imagine the map. It is the imagination that is on call here. And remember the world's wealth of languages. There is no way to make the map a felt reality if we don't speak the language in which they accessed ethical semiosis in their mother's arms. Think then how collective this wonderful call must be and how much work it entails. I feel confident that Banerjee and Wouters have thought this through.

I had to stop here because I had to talk to my somewhat post-subaltern supervisors, one scholarship student, and two assistants who are training to take my place when I'm gone. Generally we coach in math and English, but that evening we started with loving the cartographic world. As it turned out, they were all sitting on the ground, two outside a village, one in another, and the student in yet another. I began to talk about the fact that they were sitting on this great globe, hanging in space, turning so slowly that they didn't feel it, but they could measure it with a stick if the sun was shining; that they were the center, and the poles and the tropics could be measured from each of them and went on and on. But I was able to speak to them in their own local language, even using the colloquial word for backside. Much will have to be done to consolidate this imagining, to map it for today's world work, and then to imagine the time before the map, imposed on commons. Commons is maybe not hard for them to think? I cannot just claim it. But with no signage, even for villages? These are people who do not travel. And this will have to happen top and bottom, local by local—for global. Through the heart's language. An immense collective job. Writing in English, "Our words are common—battlefield din," is a desire, not its fulfillment. In the same way, if you write "Human and Other-than-Human Beings, you alone are visible Being, you alone are Real. We announce you as Right, we proclaim you as True," it would be hard to reconcile the announcer and the proclaimer as "refus[ing] … authority—expanding beyond individual positionality."

This task is an imperative today and demands almost a reversal of the affects that many wise people have told us are fundamental to the human soul—greed, fear, violence—involving the near and the far, depending.

Since my convictions in this area are well known, in asking me to write the foreword, Milinda Banerjee and Jelle Wouters have knowingly taken the chance. I would like to think that their objective is to see if I can put my money where my mouth is, and say "yes, yes" to a point of view that is not necessarily altogether my own. Our comradeship is in the requirement for a profound mind-change—rather, the rearrangement of desires—in the face of the disaster that we inhabit.

Their articulation is often aphoristic, especially toward the end, when how we (who is this "we," the implied readers?) should change ourselves is spelled out: "Relationality is assembly." "Assemblies turn the wheel of law." "Human citizenship shall be replaced by kinship of all beings. Human law overwritten by multibeing norms." "The nomad's home is Being." "Avianize territory—no state borders, and yet, self-restraint on interbeing conflict." "Through nomadism—the nostos. Through joyful hospitality to the subaltern—return to Being." "Grass is the foundation of Being." "Humans shall vegetalize." And many more.

I have included the much-abbreviated description of just the beginning of my efforts to imagine the cartographic world with a small group of recently de-subalternized subalterns to give a sense that my effort to attempt to earn the right to call forth joyful hospitality from the groups I work with is by living with and teaching at the elite level as well as the formerly subaltern level, all in all for over fifty years. Sharing a language: near-native English at the elite end and native Bengali localized at the other. I would like to think that Banerjee and Wouter's repeated statement that their project is possible is indeed a declarative suggestion that this must become possible. "I declare the war is over," sang Phil Ochs, long before the end of Vietnam. We confront the huge task of turning what they perceive into subalternity and its inherent virtues (although it does seem from a couple of asides that they know that currently these virtues are mired in historical problems). "We can learn radical democracy from the Nagas in the same way we can be inspired by the French Revolution," they write, "without admiring the Reign of Terror. Our relation to the societies we learn our pathways from is dialectical—not nostalgic."

My own work rests on a different definition of the subaltern. This pamphlet seeks to rewrite the work of the South Asian Subaltern Studies group. "Where Subaltern Studies 1.0 focused on local communities in India, Subaltern Studies 2.0 must offer pathways for heterogeneous social coalitions that ally resistant communities across the world," they write. The original Subaltern Studies group undertook to look at the role of the subaltern in the anticolonial struggles in India. In doing so, they did indeed influence the historiography of those struggles. My understanding of the subaltern goes back to Antonio Gramsci: "small social groups on the margins of history." The task is to find out how to undo this position without identity—distance from the rights and responsibilities of citizenship, and lack of access to lines of social mobility. I have spent my life attempting to destroy subalternity and insert it into the generalizability of citizenship—because the structure of the state is still the only structure available to the subaltern for resistance that reflects a general move for social justice. The state is both medicine and poison. The task is to assist in training for the medicinal dosage of the state rather than to dismantle it so that we are left with nothing but the enthusiasm of self-selected moral entrepreneurs, generally speaking and writing the imperial languages and accessing all others through translation.

This text takes all precapitalist social formations as subaltern and to an extent assumes they are full of those very precapitalist principles that would or will be able to undo our predicament. In doing so, as long as they suggest that we should learn from all social formations that have not developed capitalism, I believe they have something like a point. But to take a somewhat imaginative account of their communicative relationship with the nonhuman, as fully available today, is to contradict our deep-focus experience. And in this context the emphasis on South Asia—starting with the Nagas, and then the progressive bourgeoisie such as Rabindranath Tagore or Gandhi, as well as singular-focus citations such as from Kabir or Chandimangal, not to mention the exquisite poetry of the Upanisads—cannot be endorsed by an intellectual activist such as myself, who has been deeply critical of this very tendency among the class of South Asians going from liberal to the extreme right in India and its diaspora. It is an unexamined culturalism that offers one's own "tradition" and contemporary poetry as a model for the world even as it criticizes the original Subaltern Studies group's more analytic focus on South Asia. Certainly the subalterns I work with do not wish to resonate with efforts to rearrange their desires according to these hegemonic texts. And even the class-flattened Dalit/Bahujan community would not necessarily dance to this.

Anthony Appiah once quoted me positively, as follows: "Professor Spivak once tartly remarked, 'The question "Who should speak?" is less crucial than "Who will listen?"'"[2]

That is my question for this pamphlet. English language (and some high Bengali—the Sanskrit belongs to extremely well-known tags—and the "subaltern" languages are taken at the face value of synonyms offered by bourgeois apologists) from an elite university in Great Britain, and a Dutch anthropologist's take on Bhutan (his specialty), published in Chicago. Their readership is necessarily specific, and even then, to read is not to do. I know, as indeed I hope the pamphleteers know, that this is only the first step. If you are interested in the fully decentered global group, collected yet localized, that must be established and sustained, then you cannot cite online aboriginal languages and invoke the qualities and profundities that you can only know if you have placed yourself within the language through great intellectual effort. The simple claim between B and b in Being and being is completely unavailable to the world's diversified many-languaged ungeneralizable groups of subalterns. To produce a similar play would have to invoke a completely different set of thinking—imperfectly learned by way of a literary attachment to the subalterns. For Gramsci the relationship between the new intellectual and subalternity was one of master and disciple, where the master was the subaltern environment and the disciple the intellectual. Gramsci could not try this out, for he died, miserably sick, in political prison. But for an effort such as this one, a worldwide decentered effort on this model is in order.

I am with these two young people, hoping that they perceive that mine is an articulation, which must lead to steps that must explode their pamphlet. The aphorisms that they articulate must be "normed" in many languages in their subaltern versions, not by translation but by independent generation shared imperfectly. Their descriptions of animal communication—I was particularly taken by the invocation for human feminists to work with yak feminists—cannot simply not be anthropomorphic because they say so.

A last word for Derrida on the Nambikwara. His point was that in denying writing to them, Lévi-Strauss was not acknowledging that they were folded together with us: complicit. There was never a question of their saving the world. And the entire business about the structure of writing was to say that since speech, as articulated in this pamphlet, for example, must be meaningful in the absence of the two authors, otherwise the book should not be printed—therefore it shares the structure of writing—marks that are meaningful in the absence of the speaker. Let us not revive the old misunderstandings.

I remain strongly hopeful that this pamphlet will explode itself into the sustained responsibilities of our world and I stand to do what I can to move with the explosions, the sustainment.

The Gift of the Anthropo–not–Seen

Pluriversal Contact Zones and Speech in Translation

Marisol de la Cadena

During the last two years we have witnessed massive human death caused by a named virus—COVID-19—taking hold of the planet. Choosing to increase profit, bio-pharma did not yield intellectual patents, and both states and humanitarian institutions witnessed this but did not testify. The pandemic might of the virus was unprecedented; it intensified the destruction of life that had spread globally when, in alliance with corporate science, technology, and state coloniality, neoliberal capital occupied the earth, metabolizing into itself places it deemed unproductive, therefore empty, and ultimately *nothing*. Here I make a proposal hoping to disrupt this metabolism and its mighty destruction.

In fact, in the Americas recent decades climaxed a 500-year-long destruction that proceeded through the occupation of the bodies of kings, popes, and their acolytes by the notion of an illimitable might granted to them by God. As illimitable, therefore, should be their world reign. In the places already occupied by Christianity, the expansion violently uprooted transgressors of its limits. In what would become the Americas, Christians faced unfamiliar collectives. Using the tools of faith, proselytizers translated human-looking persons as potential prey of the devil and deserving condemnation or salvation through baptism. Christians could not think that those collectives were beyond the limits of faith because to them, there was nothing beyond those limits.

The above paragraph builds on Guha's concept of "limit" (a borrowing from Aristotle, he writes). Accordingly, the limit is "the first thing outside which there is nothing to be found, and the first thing inside which everything is to be found."[3] Interrogating "nothing" through the prism of coloniality, we may find presences that are in excess of the onto-epistemic possibilities enforced by early modern faith and modern reason of what is beyond their practices.[4] Outside the limit of what considers itself everything and crucially exceeding its onto-epistemic terms, "nothing" is.

The expansion of the Christian world did not just find a New World: it made it—in the belief that following God's Creation, persons and entities that were either human or nature were distributed as such, while continuing to be (not only human or nature), against the denial exercised by such distribution and thus excessive to it and within it. With the word "anthropo-not-seen," I make present these entities and worlding practices: they are both in excess of and through the possible offered by early modern faith and modern reason.

I learned to feel the anthropo-not-seen with Mariano Turpo, known in the southern Andes of Peru as a peasant leader who fought alongside modern leftist politicians against landowners. This depiction became insufficient when I met him. *Tirakuna* or earth beings also fought the landowners, *in inseparable relation with* Mariano.[5] This inseparability displaced many of my concepts. Mariano *with* tirakuna shocked my habit of thinking "peasant" as a human subject distinct from "land," its object. Instead, they were entangled: human and other-than-human beings, taking place—as in occurring, thus being—*together*. And what they were together was also *place*. Mariano inhabited a complex position. He confronted the state as a peasant, politically recognizable, legally claiming collectively owned peasant land. Yet tirakuna were also at trials in impossible attendance. To help me grapple with this aporia, Mariano offered the refrain I have briefly used above: *not only*. Within the limits where everything is, he was a peasant. But *not only*, because without those limits he emerged inherently with tirakuna. This human-with-other-than-human person exceeds the "subaltern peasant," yet Guha's analysis may well meet Mariano's complexities. "The politics of the people" remained "an autonomous domain," Guha wrote in his 1982 manifesto. Inhabiting this "autonomous domain," Mariano was *not only* a peasant but also a human person *with* other-than-human persons: anthropo-not-seen, a human whose being a complex person could not be, therefore not seen—or rather more clearly, not been! Contributing to Subaltern Studies 2.0, I propose that "autonomous domain" and "not only" are fellow travelers: as analytics they perform onto-epistemic openings, doorways to think what *is* without the requirements of modern thought and exceed it. Alertness to this excess may be the gift of the anthropo-not-seen toward the permanent task of decolonizing scholarly practices, including this moment of Anthropocenic deadly destruction.

Against neoliberal occupation and translation of human and other-than-human collectives into resources, "autonomous domains"—made nothing and not seen—have emerged in defense of life and through the modern possible that they also are. Examples across earth are many; I offer two from Latin America. The first one: in the Amazonian region of Ecuador a collective self-identified as Sarayaku is engaged in a legal dispute to defend their place against an oil corporation. Below is how a Sarayaku spokesperson explains their relation with what the court represented as "the territory of the Sarayaku people," where the corporation had buried explosives:

> The state (…) indicated that an explosive is dangerous when it is attached to a human body: that is classification A. Classification B is when an explosive is left in a building; (…) you can evacuate people. [C]lassification C is when explosives are somewhere far away. The state said that the presence of explosives in

Sarayaku falls into category C because they're far from the main dwelling place of Sarayaku people and they don't present a threat; hence, there is no need to remove them. But for us their presence represents category A, and that is what we told the state: that *the explosives are attached to the body of the Sarayaku.*[6]

My emphasis in the last sentence wants us to read its complexity. As territory Sarayaku can be mapped into three-dimensional coordinates as the court suggested, *and not only*: Sarayaku is also *kawsay sacha*. This Indigenous name translates as "living forest"—what Sarayaku is: persons human and other than human taking place inherently together, inseparable into "humans," "plants," "animals," and "territory," their presence exceeding classification as bios and geos, life and nonlife. In Sarayaku, explosives are buried in kawsay sacha, a place inseparable into territories and bodies.

My second example concerns the Atrato River, running across the northwestern Colombia rainforest named Chocó. In 2016 Atrato acquired constitutional personhood: its rights (considered biological) became linked to the rights (considered biocultural) of the Indigenous and Afro-Colombian people who live with it. The constitutional ruling emerged from an alliance (against gold mining) between constitutional lawyers and local environmentalists, among them a group organized as "cuerpo guardianes del Atrato," in English, "guardian bodies of the Atrato." Luz Enith Mosquera, an Atrato guardian, explains,

> The law formalized *what we have always been, the Atrato*. As guardians we defend the river we are, its territory which is us: bodies defending the life of all the bodies we are. Our umbilical cords are buried here; we have roots, like the trees, and nobody can sever the ties. It is hard to understand, but we do not defend what is *there*, an object; we defend what we are, ourselves, the Atrato, a collective deciding autonomously our development without the neoliberal imposed vision. The Atrato legal personhood is a door to understand that *we are* the Atrato River.[7]

In earlier work I have suggested that rejecting subject/object and culture/nature distinctions—listen to: "*we are* the Atrato River"—may *uncommon nature*.[8] Analogous to the human but not only anthropo-not-seen, when place is an entanglement of humans with nature, the latter emerges as specifically local, uncommon to the usual (universal) abstraction that science can know, the state can legislate, and the market can appropriate. Yet also appearing through them (because otherwise they are not), these events may display pluriversal occasions: when worlding practices (and entities) deemed impossible in the modern domain disrupt it and present themselves reclaiming possibility against the limits that denied them and obliged their being as nothing.[9]

Years ago, Mary Louise Pratt used the term "contact zones" to conceptualize the space and processes through which divergent worlds encountered each other and composed pidgin conditions of being, including languages, all articulated by "radical asymmetrical relations of power."[10] Exploring this last phrase, I qualify Pratt's concept with the term "pluriversal" to open possibility to presences that *were and continue to be* beyond the limits of the onto-epistemic power that deemed them nothing. Being where and what nothing could be, yet displaying grammars imposed upon them, these presences created ontic pidgins that housed what could be and *not only*. Pluriversal contact zones are a complexity: ecologies of divergent self-asserting presences and worlding practices that inflect and exceed each other, where the (pluriversal) excess may go unfelt as it emerges beyond the (universal, even if local) limits of the modern possible. The anthropo-not-seen or uncommon nature, entangled with each other, excessive to the human distinct from nature, and emerging through negativities against their denial. As may be obvious to the reader, coloniality is also a dynamic in this ecology.

Pluriversal contact zones are everywhere, interrupting modern practices of all kinds: the courts and a film as Sarayaku did, law and mining as did the Atrato River. The event through which I initially thought pluriversal contact zones happened in Cuzco (Peru) in defense of Ausangate, a mountain *and* an earth being. Gathered around this complex, self-excessive entity and allied against a potential gold mine were Indigenous activists defending the earth being and urban environmentalists defending the mountain and ignoring the earth being. Aware of the discrepancy, the Indigenous activists chose to continue in the alliance: Ausangate would be better protected as a mountain whose destruction would have environmental consequences than as an earth being whose disappearance would have unknown effects in local worlds. The alliance was an environmental success *and* an onto-epistemic tool that smothered Ausangate as earth being. That those who cared for it also prevented its excessive presence from appearing in public is not a historical surprise: earth beings are hegemonically impossible; their presence could have been a hindrance even among well-intentioned environmentalists.[11] Pluriversal contact zones are uncertain as political terrain; canceling being beyond its limits, the onto-epistemic closet may smother excess as it comes out, transform it into what it accepts (a cultural belief?), and force it to endure on the outskirts of the modern possible. This may happen benevolently, like in the above case, through environmentalism. But then, pluriversal contact zones are also arenas where colonial onto-epistemic denials are themselves denied by presences that forcefully and publicly assert themselves, to wit: we are the Atrato, we do not defend what is there, we defend what we are, and also loudly speaking the impossible in the courts, "the explosives are attached to the body of the Sarayaku."

Pluriversal contact zones are an ecology of pidgin speeches that invite us to slow down our scholarly categories and grammars and what they may listen to, and thus make our ears (and other senses) capable of listening to what our analytics (tools of hegemonic epistemic mandates) may not feel or know how to express: for example, persons and place inseparably together. Scholarly attunement with pluriversal contact zones also requires considering speech in permanent translation, aware that what we hear or say may not mean what it also means. Davi Kopenawa Yanomami offers an example. As a guest in innumerable international fora—pluriversal contact zones for attendees capable of multiworlding understandings—Davi Kopenawa addresses his audiences in Portuguese, stating that he uses it because it is the language that the public (or the translator) can understand. He consequently warns that the meanings of his words in Portuguese are in translation from the Yanomami language and may not necessarily match what the audience will hear; however, enough communication will be established for a conversation to be possible. One of the words that he frequently explains is "spirit," *espírito* in Portuguese: he learned the word to tell non-Yanomami (Brazilians and others) that what he knows comes from being with-through *xapiri*—inhabitants of the forests. "Spirit" and xapiri are not the same, but the words allow conversation and some understanding of xapiri that, however, modern audiences need to control to avoid colonial practices of equivocation[12] that would translate "spirit" as uttered by Davi Kopenawa into modern relations of belief and xapiri into not being. Doing this would cancel the excessive presences that Davi Kopenawa summons to the conversation. Perhaps Mariano's refrain could help avoid such translation: modern audiences can think spirit and *not only*, also xapiri. Moderns would not know what *is* what inhabits the possibility opened to it through "not only," but feeling the excess through this refrain may suspend the power granted to modern onto-epistemic stances to make nothing what *is* beyond their limits.

Excessive presences can make pluriversal contact zones tangible; they suggest an unknown togetherness in which worlds must learn to live, paying pragmatic attention to the coloniality of practices that made the world one. Dauntingly impossible as this may feel, its undertaking may match in reverse the feeling as a beyond-the-ordinary decolonial endeavor. Making our scholarly senses vulnerable to a shock, we may find ourselves in the presence of uncommon nature and anthropo-not-seen, a world of many worlds asserting their being across pluriversal contact zones and stubbornly refusing to live within the limits of the onto-epistemic separation between human and nature. If historically the coloniality of this separation allowed the anthropo-seen to appropriate what it deemed nature or make "nothing" collectives that *were* beyond its limits, such coloniality currently emerges from its own genealogy with a combination of mighty technoscientific power and limitless greed for wealth that threatens to extinguish the lives of all planetary collectives, including its own.

Animal Lessons

Thom van Dooren

Other species arguably have much to teach us about how to live well on this planet. One of the central threads of this manifesto for Subaltern Studies 2.0 is a turn toward the more-than-human world, and to other animals in particular, for the insights they might offer as "primal instructors of humans." In its pages, we learn about how various modes of social life, from marriage and monogamy to territoriality, democracy, and the ethics of nonviolence, might be understood as lessons imparted to humanity through observation of the behaviors of animal others. Through these examples we see something of the diversity—cultural, historical, and geographical—of these ways of thinking with animals about human life. We also get a sense of the many terrains—including sexuality, ethics, and political and familial structures—into which animal life might provide insight. But perhaps most productively of all, these examples open up important questions about the *status* of these lessons. What precisely do they teach and who decides? How should they be received? What authority do they travel with and why?

My short comment is an effort to sketch my own response to this provocation. My position is that while spending time with animals in this way offers potential for insight, it also carries significant dangers. Although

animals are sometimes positioned as guides, instructors, or teachers, my sense is that they might better be
understood as something akin to *interlocutors*. Which
is to say that what other animal species offer us are not
readily transferable lessons, and certainly not models for
human life, but a diversity of modes of being that might
be thought with and against, explored and queried, in an
effort both to understand ourselves better and to more
creatively and generously hold open room in the world for
others.

My approach to thinking with the social worlds
of other animals about what it means to be human is
grounded in a few key considerations.

First, nonhuman animals are a diverse bunch. If you
look hard enough you can find an example "in nature" to
make pretty much any kind of argument you like. If you
want to advocate for monogamy, then the avian world
is probably your best bet (provided you don't look too
closely). If you're after examples of same-sex sexual inter-
actions, then the hedgehogs have some fascinating behaviors to consider.[13] If you're in favor of clear hierarchies
held in place by violent force, then, according to some at
least, baboons might just be your guys. When it comes to
political life, honeybees have long been a prized example,
generally demonstrating the value of a well-ordered
society ruled by a benevolent monarch. Of course, for all
of these examples there are other species that might speak
in favor of the opposite arrangements, or at least vastly

different ones. And as we'll see, these are far from the only stories that might be told about these particular creatures.

Second, even once we've settled on what seems to be an ideal—or convenient?—animal example, significant challenges persist in the interpretive lenses that we bring to animal social worlds. At the end of the day, the lessons that we take from animals are as much about projecting our own values, practices, and politics onto them as they are about "finding" examples out there. As Cynthia Chris notes in her discussion of animal documentaries, this projection can be more or less intentional: "The wildlife genre in particular, and the extra-media discourses that inform it, are sites of both purposeful ideological work and unconscious elaboration of beliefs so normalized as common sense—about nature, animals, race, gender, sexuality, economic and political formations—that they may not be recognized (by filmmakers, by television programmers, by scientists, by audiences) as ideological." This is a dynamic that we see play out again and again in wildlife documentaries: from the US Cold War–era films that emphasized survival of the fittest in a way that neatly dovetailed with dominant liberal ideologies of individualism and nationalism[14] to the documentaries made during the Third Reich that drew analogies between the "social efficiency of animal species [like bees and ants] and the German fascist state," in which every individual knows and unquestioningly takes up their allotted role.[15] As historian Julia Kindt has noted, this is just one of the many political lives that honeybees have had, being variously invoked in support of feudalism, mercantilism, communism, fascism, the papacy, and more.[16]

Third, these efforts to understand and extract meaning from animal social worlds are further complicated by the fact that their multiplicity is not simply a question of interpretive lenses. Different individuals and social cohorts within species do actually live differently, and in ways that are not static or fixed. In recent years some of the intraspecific diversity in the social lives of animals has been studied under the rubric of "animal culture." Through this research we have learned about a variety of behaviors, in all sorts of species, that pass between generations through social learning and so are frequently not shared by all members of the species but confined to a particular population. Examples range from the specific regional song dialects of many bird species and the unique practice of one group of bottlenose dolphins who use sponges to aid their foraging, through to the many distinctive traditions of tool use, communication, grooming, and even tickling found among Africa's chimpanzee communities.[17]

Most of these studies focus on a particular behavior, but occasionally we also get glimpses of a broader cultural milieu *in the making*. One of my favorite examples concerns a troop of baboons living on the Serengeti. This troop had been studied since the 1970s and found to have what was then generally considered a "typical" social culture for their species: extremely hierarchical and ordered through high rates of male aggression. While females were frequently involved in affiliative behaviors, male-male affiliation was said to be "nonexistent." Then something happened. Through a strange series of events, in the early 1980s most of the more aggressive males were accidentally poisoned. In the years that followed, the social dynamics of the troop were transformed. According to Robert Sapolsky, who studied them at the time: "The new social milieu involved a 'relaxed' dominance style (less displacement aggression directed at females and subordinate males by dominant males), more tolerance by dominant males of occasional dominance reversals by subordinates, more inter-sexual grooming and closer proximity among animals."[18] In the years that followed, this new style endured, with all of the males who subsequently joined or were born into the group being enculturated into this mode of baboon sociality.

Here we see that species are not singular or fixed modes of life. Of course, this is true across the long multigenerational time frames that we sometimes call "evolutionary." But animals are also innovating new modes of life on smaller scales, learning to exploit new resources or to live differently with one another. In some cases, these innovations are passed on through processes of social learning and might ultimately have profound consequences for the evolution of the species—or even the emergence of a new one. For our purposes here, however, the point is, yet again, that there is no singular way of life of a given species, and so there are no simple lessons to be drawn from them.

But it is from precisely this assumed timelessness and singularity of the ways of life of baboons, bees, or dolphins that much of the rhetorical force of these animal lessons is derived. This situation brings us to the fourth, final, and most important reason we should carefully interrogate efforts to find answers applicable to human life in the practices of other members of the animal kingdom. Put simply, there is no good reason any other animal should provide authoritative insight into human life. Even if all other animals organized themselves after a singular, unchanging pattern, this would provide no justification for assuming that we should do so too. To think otherwise is to make an at best logically dubious "appeal to nature."[19]

These kinds of appeals are grounded in the strange stamp of authority that nature is often thought to provide. The presence of a particular social configuration among some group of animals gives it a legitimacy that it would not have if the same configuration were simply presented as a speculative possibility. The basis for the authority of nature is shifting and diverse: it might come by virtue of divine creation, nature's postulated inherent harmony and balance, or its functioning via universal laws; or even be imagined to have been granted via the grand sifting processes of evolution by natural selection.[20]

In the Western world, the rhetorical force of this position has long been grounded in a dualized understanding in which humans are positioned outside "nature" in a world of "culture." In such a context, other animals—who are generally assumed, contrary to the evidence, not to "have culture"—can provide a window into this more authentic and pure state of nature.

Of course, the flip side of this appeal to nature as an ideal is the ever-present possibility that what is natural is positioned instead as lowly, dirty, and in need of civilizing. The many groups of humans who have found themselves positioned as "closer to nature" have frequently experienced the impacts of this oscillation between their romanticization and denigration. The same charged selectivity exists in assessments of nonhuman animal life as natural or not. As James D. Weinrich has succinctly put it, "When animals do something that we like we call it natural. When they do something that we don't like, we call it animalistic."[21] We see this, for example, in the responses to the widespread same-sex sexual activity of diverse animal species: used by some to argue that homosexuality is natural and by others to argue that it is a base part of our "bestial nature" that must be transcended. Both arguments are highly dubious[22] ultimately showing only the extreme flexibility and capacity for co-optation of what is counted as nature in any given context.[23]

Despite these kinds of objections, animal lessons continue to be called on in this way. As this Manifesto makes clear, this practice has a deep history and diverse cultural forms. It can be operationalized against modes of intrahuman oppression, as with the use of models of animal democracy by anticolonial intellectuals in India in the late-nineteenth and early twentieth century "to condemn the colonial state and call for democratization among humans" (p. 82). But it can just as often, perhaps more often, be used in the opposite way, to reinforce existing dominant ideologies and assumptions.

To suggest we be wary of animal lessons and the strange authority they carry is not to say that we should simply ignore them. They have much to teach us. At the broadest level, paying attention to other animals as social and even cultural beings draws us into a world of evolutionary continuities. It reminds us, as Dominique Lestel has put it, of the "animal origins of human culture."[24] These continuities produce stories that are always simultaneously ones of sameness and difference. To attend to both—to learn to see what we share with others and what makes each of us unique—is the basis not only of any mature and informed sense of self but also of any genuinely ethical relationship.[25] This requires us to engage thoughtfully with other animal ways of life on their own terms, to appreciate them for their profound possibilities and their limitations within the particular contexts where they have arisen and now endure (or don't). This is what I have referred to as treating other animals as *interlocutors*. Animals are not one-dimensional or static, they are not selectively chosen sources of (questionable) authority for ideological positions. Rather they are complex living beings who will not conform to our stories and must instead be given "the power to oblige [us] to think."[26] In some cases, other animals will provide glimpses of insight into how we perhaps should or shouldn't organize our own modes of life. But these will never be simple models to be emulated or avoided. At best they will be windows into other worlds that might be the basis for careful, critical reflection and dialogue.

But there is another, I think more interesting and important, lesson that we might take from animals. In this time of extinctions, as so many species and so many diverse modes of life are slipping out of the world, to attend to others' ways of being is to enrich and deepen our sense of what is being lost. At the same time, learning more about others—not as caricatured morality tales but as actual living beings—opens up avenues for imagining new modes of cohabitation. It is here that paying attention to how animals live might offer us the most important lessons about how we should live. Not as models to be emulated, but as modes of life that when carefully considered and appreciated on their own terms allow us to ask in ever more nuanced ways: What would it take for us to hold open or create room in the world for these others to endure and flourish?

Supreme Subalterns

Suraj Yengde

The idea of the individual as a being smothered in multiplicities is taken as a point of departure in the lyrical dancing of
this manifesto—Subaltern Studies 2.0. The call is extended
to those people whose names we might have heard before,
or not. But the call becomes a whisper of justice.

I read this draft in the mountains of the Balkans
and the terrain of the UAE. The Balkans were broken into
pieces for gains of tribalism against the unity of those
resisting the agenda that this pamphlet advocates. The
UAE, on the other hand, managed to sustain tribalism for
national sovereignty.

Various experiences across the world speak to similar
stories of a unified rise of neoliberal capitalism. The geog-
raphy and the culprit, unlike the past century, are living
among us. Capitalism has changed its color, caste, and
identity to assimilate into our common beings. It has
become part of our consciousness, an extremely dangerous move that has not only normalized its presence in our
societies but also made it indispensable. It has taken the
name of innovation, technology, ideas, culture, sports,
democracy, and human rights and used all the correct
symbols.

It has made itself the superman, or now superwoman,
trying to save the world from the unknown catastrophe.

Popular fiction and sci-fi elicit our immediate fears and allow us to peek into the old age's human desires—cultish and divisive. These genres also send an indirect message to think about extraterrestrial beings. It is a dog whistle to the temperament of the nerdy, who are trained to launch adventures in the colonizing of non-Earth spaces by humans.

Talking about humans as a singular noun is a fallacy. Popular struggles try to use this optimist identity as if every human will join their agitprop. We need to distinguish among humans and emphasize the uniqueness of the divides that neoliberal capitalism has now amplified beyond bounds. Humans make up an interconnected species, differentiated from others by a heightened consciousness capable of achieving liberation. That makes everyone qualified to seek the final goal in their present moment.

Enter "Diversity" Capitalism

In an airplane bound to cross over a continent in several hours, one notices children six to seven years old occupying business-class seats while octogenarians huddle in the cramped seats that afford once-in-a-lifetime travel for the middle class of Eastern European nations. The postcommunist bloc of Yugoslavia does not try hard to distinguish the betrayal of Europe from that of the West. At the same time, it wants to benefit from the pragmatism of the Western empire that lives in the stories of a glorious past.

Even though the Western dream lured these socialists into thinking about common goals of development for their children, they're still second-class passengers in the long queue of capitalism's gains. As they pass toward their designated spot in the back of the aircraft after a long time waiting—at the check-in counter, at security, at the final check-in point, in the jetway, and inside the aircraft—they are accepting the assurances of being continually kept in waiting. When they enter, the differentiated class that breezed through with elite access is already sipping their drinks. No one color or nationality is dominating the coveted seats. In the business of exploitation, everyone has a stake.

What then is the role of diversity in a project of liberation? Diversity validates the existence of systems. It balances an act of rejection or exploitation. The gains from corporate exploits are channeled into trust funds and charity foundations that get dissolved into social movements. The popular, media-savvy crowd gets recognized as representatives of the people and their cause. Democracy is traded as a symbol of faith. It fits into the narrative of a panacea applied to every political problem. Therefore, the lovers of democracy buy into the logic of its liberal capitalism. Unknowingly, the victim of the system becomes a participant in it. Votes get mixed with emotion. Fanaticism takes birth. Self-righteousness becomes an end goal and vanity a truthful ordeal. In this mayhem, a possible answer is the directive to more diverse hiring in the chamber of exploitation. The diverse candidate is then ordered to implement the rule of capital's law. If they cannot or will not, they are declared incompetent and unfit. Either way, capitalism triumphs, and the individuals supporting it retain the historical position of power and oppression.

Person of Color Capitalism

The neoliberal order has received an extension on life, which has made it a cultural program for the world to embrace through promising symbolism. What are the markers or symbols? They can be categorized in three ways: signal birthing of righteousness, identity as politics, and intraclass war as a measure of justice.

The era of policies decided by the metropole is no longer as clear. The men in positions of power who gained a say in the world reorganization are still there, but there has also been a rise of so-called colored national men and women who are now occupying the seats in the executive chambers of the IMF and the World Bank, drafting policies for new loans. These jobs are presented to the younger generation as glamorous and coveted. The IMF chief being an Indian or a nonwhite Westerner undoes the work of liberation. It replaces tokenized representation with complete reformation.

The reformation has been extended to the techno-capital enterprises acting as imperialism's loyal pets, located in various metropoles with regional office heads in formerly colonized countries. The model of Google, Facebook, Netflix, and many other billion-dollar companies has altered the reality of humans with a metaverse. Lives have been further atomized to chatting and living in a world of communications. The CEOs of major American corporations are of dominant castes, including Sundar Pichai (Brahmin) of Google, Satya Nadella (Brahmin) of Microsoft, Parag Agarwal (Bania) of Twitter, Arvind Krishan (Brahmin) of IBM, V.K. Narasimhan (Brahmin) of Novartis, and D.C. Paliwal (Bania) of Harman, among others.

American capitalism validates historical oppressions in the garb of merit and talent. Those with a pedigree of privilege and unaccounted support qualify for the tests to enter Western higher education. The segue from non-Western English-medium schools to Western degree programs to corporate positions is set already. Thus, putting the burden of blame on the West or neoliberal capitals is an incomplete argument. We need to identify the agents of neoliberalism that act as middlemen/women to complete their tasks.

During the times of indentured labor, laborers exported from India were Dalit and Shudra, and the middlemen were shopkeepers—the Bania, and upper Shudra acting as in-between capitalists, profited from the miseries imposed by the imperial order on African and Dalit laborers. As in this historical trajectory, the Indian caste elite finds its place in twenty-first-century imperialism, yet again a diverse candidate. There cannot be a singular focus of oppression; it is intersectional. Corporate executives of color also impose oppression and have to be accountable for it.

Beingness

The affectionate appraisal of the nonhuman body is one of the wonderful responses this new collective imagination aims to proffer. It raises the consciousness of the subject and the subjugated. The erstwhile objectified nonhuman is also a human now. In this age where animals increasingly have rights without having to argue in the courts, the legal world is considering whether an animal is a person. Nonhuman beings are regarded as things without good life or value. This approach stems from humans' victory over the animal kingdom in the struggle for survival.

Animal subjugation is one way to justify human arrogance over nonhuman beings declared "beasts." Relegation of the animal personality to an unconscious being rationalizes the cruelty and denigration of the nonhuman. They occupy the lowest position in the vertical hierarchy of the food chain, proving that the perception of interaction with beasts persists in humans' minds.

Indian approaches to nonhuman life have often been extreme, either worship or condemnation. There rarely was any middle path to reckon with this dilemma. In 2013, the government of India declared dolphins and orcas "nonhuman persons ... with their own specific rights." There is a story behind this. It has to do with the rise of beings' consciousness, appreciated and preserved in the Dalit community. Animals and plants are what Sajan Mani calls "our nonhuman ancestors."

There is hardly a difference between reincarnation and the myth of rebirth. But finding connections and extensions of faith, love, and tears with unspeaking beings has not replaced the animal with the human but made the animal appear in its original form. The new types of breeds created for the pleasure of humans through difficult cross-breeding between pets have a short life and a painful ordeal as animals acting as grown people's toys.

Nonhuman beings have been fancied the alter ego of the human. This fiction validated cruelty and its disastrous effects upon animals. Humans' rights are a-species. They do not have an intimate link with the ecology of the environment. Others' dependability is a crucial component of our collective survival. However, capitalism separated humans into various groups and further distanced our relationship with fellow species. To normalize this, cruelty to nonhuman beings was made a fashion: whether the food in fine restaurants, high-priced apparel commodities, or rhino horns used for drugs to maintain erections, we've attempted to find taste in everything as the great sage, Kabir noted.

A history of animality accorded to the status of beings is not new to Dalits. Animals were part of their minds and bodies. They lived among them, at times as affectionate companions but most of the time forced to adjust as animals had to. A Savarna caste Hindu landlord would not want his fiefs to share anything that would raise the consciousness of respect and dignity—essential for human beings to know their agency. The grandfather of Bandhu Madhav was a serf who begged for work from the landlord. The caste-loving landlord imposed a determinant humiliation on this elderly person. Bandhu Madhav, a young child, witnessed this denigration. His grandfather was forced to eat the grain fed to the cattle. That was the compensation a Dalit deserved after toiling for the whole day, "poisoned bread," toxic and indigestible. The food that nonhuman beings ate was also a staple for Dalits, albeit without choice.

There was hardly a difference between a Dalit and an animal. They were forced to live alongside each other. They relied on each other, became responsive to each other's unspoken words but loud emotions. They cared and nurtured their present moments. A Dalit was meant to be a beast, his identity supposedly attached to the strength of a bovine. He was condemned. His last name was changed from the rulers of the native land to that of the animals. The oppressor casteists ensured that no hint of historical pride remained. Thus, Dalit last names—Dhore (buffalo), Kolhe (wolf), Dukre (pig), Pandi (pig), Gurram (horse)— are epithets of historical violence and reduced infancy attributed to their Being. This provided legitimacy to the violent actions of the casteist lord, who whipped these people without remorse as he would cattle in scorching sunlight.

The Dalit animality, however, was desired by the men and women of the caste lords. The women lusted after

Dalit men, seducing the subordinated and encouraging them to take risks to satisfy them. Many children born to the caste lords had a genetic pool of Dalit blood.

The nonhuman being is also the everyday flora. The trees, plants, and vegetation are all recognized, appreciated as responsible beings in their life. Dalits cannot imagine a location without identifying the markers of nature. The mountains, trees, and glaciers are all part of a history that is deep and interconnected. Nature is a symbol of worship, a totem of fear, a memory from the past. It is a cure, an elder that offers shade and medicine. There is an intrinsic quality to it. My father encouraged us to plant trees on our birthdays and grow with them like our child or a friend. This was a meeting point of tradition and acknowledgment of the interchange among earthly beings. The interchange is multidirectional, but it is anchored in a politics of the local, the true self. Winds of many seasons and cultures can come and participate in the ceremonies of the local, but the tree remains true to its position. The Dalit identifies with the rootedness of everyone. Everyone is from somewhere.

The State and Its Priestly Machinations

The bold statement in the manifesto calls for dismantling power structures inherited through the colonial edifice of control and implemented by the sovereign government of the nation-state. However, the focus is on capital as a centerpiece of this mayhem. The authors leave us with further questions. What is the nature of postcapital society? "Nature" here refers to the extraction of resources, primarily exploiting the environment and the people who live by it. And what is the nonstate or a-state entity going to look like?

Many would pursue an agenda of the tribal form of governance, or assemblies of kinships that have a workable democracy but confined to a lineage-ascended monarchy. After all, the leaders of the anticolonial struggle across the world had prestige and status as the upperclass, dominant caste that gave them the advantage in claiming their rights to leadership and freedom. Almost no one is separate from the regulated hierarchy that warrants the privilege of consciousness. This consciousness provided a political mandate to the local elites, who turned against the oppressors. One cannot deny the relative advantage such a political mandate offered to the native class.

The structure of the colonial architecture is different from the structure that existed in precolonial times, and so is the colonial chronotope. Does the colonial mandate begin only when Europeans start to expand on caste, race, and capital logic across the world, or does an empire exist before it? Take, for example, South Asia. Ottoman rulers were clubbed with other Central Asian Muslim rulers alongside the Mongols who found their way into this vast land. Their project was also exploitation of labor and collection of revenue. However, these differed from the totality of extraction meant to feed the market in the colonial capital center—the metropoles.

The poetic eclecticism of this manifesto is a treatment of the natural flow of ideas. After all, the world is written down in poesis. History is a poem, and so is the cure to the illness. One cannot expect to be hard-edged, geometrically angled, when approaching the topic of faithfulness. If the world needs practice, it needs a sonic language. The musicality of communication rests on the temperament of the speaker and listener. One has to be on the level of hearing before speaking. Thus, the old age adage is about simplicity. Modern science has subverted simplicity into unnecessary verbosity. The most challenging thing for a human is the desire to conquer death. Ancient wisdom tried explaining the limitation of life and death. Yet, with the sermonic advantage of the education that migrated into the academic canons, we are doomed to the hubris of average human beings trying to pretend we are someone other than the simple, stripped, naked self.

This text in discussion is suspicious of the state. It anchors its principal analysis on the stateism of the political economy. The critique is directed toward unequally held authority and not distributive relations of power. Sovereignty and capital—two interconnected, separated twins that gave rise to individualism, greed, and profanity—converge into a market dead zone. The authors call this a practice of communicating with the dead—necromancy. This supposes that we are already at a point on a time scale that is a moment of death if seen through the lens of the future, looking backward to our present moment. A dystopia of the Anthropocene feared by all, averted by none.

The exhortation offered in this treatise reads as the clairvoyance of deeply caring humans. It is a beautiful rendition of thoughts to be faced.

One of the totemic fears of a worldy call to action is juxtaposing frameworks with concepts. The identities are macro, and the heterogeneity among them, sometimes violent co-survival, gets a pass. If the Muslim in India has to be categorized, there has to be a democratic charter of social identity opposed to the binary, historically homogenous caliphate identities reincarnated in the twenty-first century as minorities of the world. This process refuses the global character of the varieties of Islam, an imperial tactic to ghettoize the believers of one Abrahamic faith. Colonial incompetency decides the behavior and mannerisms of the ruling class in a new phase of modernity.

A possible move out of this is perhaps the guidance of the fully enlightened one. The Buddha is a reason for experiences. His ways are human and politically expedient. The new collective faithfully relies on these experiences that transcend the limitation of humans, religions, cults, God, and hell.

A New Subaltern?

The focus is still limited to humans' profligacy with everything in their ecology, where the earth is a bed of exploitation. She needs to be abused for the greed of a few to manipulate all into self-destruction. The space for space and the human desire to colonize the extraterrestrial are sponsored by the states. So, the call of this manifesto is indeed realistic. It squares the debacle of the power and play performed in the petri dish of the state. The war on earth and indeed the rush toward the extraterrestrial are predicated on consumer citizenship, where each and every one has to carry a value, without which they may not even see the light.

The subaltern studies collective was inspired by the Gramscian doctrine of the lower classes, the powerless yet unifying culture of society. Subaltern studies focused on the collective identity of the peasant, creating a global language of the struggles of the lower classes. These collaborations in a global class identity provided the desired attention to the Indian scholars responsible for the collective. However, they missed the chance to offer a Gramscian probe into the question of the Indian subaltern—the Dalit and Adivasi. Brahmin, Kayastha, and Ashraf Mussalman scholars from the subcontinent and white progressives from the West joined in this rallying cry of scholarship activism.

I asked subaltern studies scholars, postcolonial scholars, and activists of the Global South where to fit the story of the Dalit. Everyone had a confessional tone of culpability when replying that it wouldn't easily fit anyplace. Gayatri Spivak suggested that Dalits appropriate the category of the subaltern, as it was originally directed toward Dalits. Gramsci had Dalits in mind when he would categorize subaltern identity, she claimed. I confronted this dilemma in the last decade. Where do I place the human quality of Dalit in the well-intentioned but incomplete global experiences of the aforementioned categories? The answer is clear: Dalits are all of the above, and yet they are not the same. They are working class, peasants, poor, subaltern. However, they're not only class categories. They're empowered in their spiritual traditions. They are not victims of a moment; their enforced oppression is temporally expansive.

Dalits are not neatly organized groups of colonial categories. They cannot easily fit the descriptions. Identifying them in the logic of capitalism allows diversity and the noncolonial, modern capitalistic experience to wash them away. It eliminates the contradictory fission of the personal, social, community, and cultural avenues of self-development. That is why subaltern cannot be a sole option to these groups. Still, they were made what I have called elsewhere "subordinate subalterns," i.e., their experiences were not privileged enough to be categorized by the collective. Dalits can be subalterns, but they are captains of their destiny. They do not live in the paradox of binarism. Like the walking Buddha, they are on the path toward collective enlightenment enshrined in Ambedkar's Navayana Buddhism.

Walking is an action. It demands that people do the act rather than idly not. Ambedkar is for the movement of a singular body that when enacted has the possibility to inspire others to join the call. This collection brings in energies of multiplicities. Each piece brings the spirit of courage and goose bump-worthy attention to the call. Force, adoration, and deliberation bring to the fore the bareness of life. In this call, life has much as detail as nonlife. After all, they are related and rely upon each other.

Notes

1. Please consult Vijay Prashad, "In the Name of Saving the Climate They Will Uberise the Farmland: The Forty-Sixth Newsletter" (2021), Tricontinental: Institute for Social Research, for an example of the spectralization of land. Examples are everywhere. https://thetricontinental.org/newsletterissue/agricultural-technology/.

2. A version of this article appeared in print on August 12, 2018, Section SR, p. 1 of the New York edition with the headline: "Speaking as a ..."

3. Guha 2003, 7.

4. A corollary of this thought would be that what considers itself everything cannot know or feel what it denies, even if being with it (see de la Cadena 2021).

5. The Quechua word for this relation is *ayllu*: it names the insep-arability of human and other-than-human persons as they take place. In Spanish ayllu becomes *comunidad campesina*, a word that names a relation of separation between place (land) and people. See de la Cadena 2015.

6. In the film *Forest Law/Selva Juridica* (2014), by Ursula Biemann and Paulo Tawares, https://vimeo.com/114999421.

7. Round Table Virtual Series, *Celebrating 20 Years of the Working Group: Making Sense of Political Ecology in Abya-Ayala*, second meeting, "The Commons Viewed from Southern Political Ecologies," panelists: Luz enith Mosquera, Marisol de la Cadena, Arturo Escobar, April 10, 2022, https://www.youtube.com/watch?v=xWmJdIvwcIM.

8. For "uncommon nature" see de la Cadena 2019.

9. Another caveat, this time for those dismissive of the localized as "micro": these events suspend modern impossibilities; the challenge posed is conceptual and defies scalability.

10. Pratt 2007, 7.

11. About this see "The Politics of Modern Politics Meets Ethnographies of Excess Through Ontological Openings," Society for Cultural Anthropology, January 13, 2014, https://culanth.org/fieldsights/the-politics-of-modern-politics-meets-ethnographies-of-excess-through-ontological-openings.

12. Viveiros de Castro 2004.

13. Bruce Bagemihl, *Biological Exuberance: Animal Homosexuality and Natural Diversity* (New York: St. Martin's Press, 1999).

14. Cynthia Chris, *Watching Wildlife* (Minneapolis: University of Minnesota Press, 2006), 37.

15. Jan-Christopher Horak, "Wildlife Documentaries: From Classical Forms to Reality TV," *Film History: An International Journal* 18, no. 4 (2006): 465.

16. Julia Kindt, *The Trojan Boar and Other Stories: 10 Ancient Creatures That Make Us Human* (forthcoming).

17. Lucy M. Aplin, "Culture and Cultural Evolution in Birds: A Review of the Evidence," *Animal Behaviour* 147 (2019): 179–87. Michael Krützen, Janet Mann, Michael R. Heithaus, Richard C. Connor, Lars Bejder, and William B. Sherwin, "Cultural Transmission of Tool Use in Bottlenose Dolphins," *Proceedings of the National Academy of Sciences* 102, no. 25 (2005): 8939–43. Andrew Whiten and Christophe Boesch, "The Cultures of Chimpanzees," *Scientific American* 284, no. 1 (2001): 60-67.

18. Robert M. Sapolsky, "Culture in Animals: The Case of a Non-Human Primate Culture of Low Aggression and High Affiliation," *Social Forces* 85 (2006): 225.

19. Bonnie Steinbock, "The Appeal to Nature," in *The Ideal of Nature: Debates About Biotechnology and the Environment*, edited by Gregory E. Kaebnick (Baltimore: Johns Hopkins University Press, 2011), 98-113.

20. Lorraine Daston and Fernando Vidal, eds., *The Moral Authority of Nature* (Chicago: University of Chicago Press, 2003).

21. Cited in Myra J. Hird, "Animal Trans," in *Queering the Non/human*, edited by Noreen Giffney and Myra J. Hird (London and New York: Routledge, 2016), 227.

22. Stacy Alaimo, "Eluding Capture: The Science, Culture, and Pleasure of 'Queer' Animals," in *Queer Ecologies: Sex, Nature, Politics, Desire*, edited by Catriona Mortimer-Sandilands and Bruce Erickson (Bloomington: Indiana University Press, 2010), 51-72.

23. Donna Haraway, *Primate Visions: Gender, Race, and Nature in the World of Modern Science* (New York and London: Routledge, 1989).

24. Dominique Lestel, *Les Origines Animales De La Culture* (Paris: Flammarion, 2003).

25. Val Plumwood, *Feminism and the Mastery of Nature* (London and New York: Routledge, 1993).

26. Isabelle Stengers, "The Cosmopolitical Proposal," in *Making Things Public: Atmospheres of Democracy*, edited by Peter Weibel and Bruno Latour (Cambridge and Karlsruhe: MIT Press, 2005), 998.

Select References

Ali, Salim. *The Book of Indian Birds*. Bombay: The Bombay Natural History Society, 1941.

Ambedkar, B. R. *The Essential Writings of B. R. Ambedkar*. Edited by Valerian Rodrigues. Delhi: Oxford University Press, 2002.

Ap Chuni Dorji. "Yak Legpai Lhadar Gawo." Translated with the help of Thinley Dema.

Agamben, Giorgio. *The Kingdom and the Glory: For a Theological Genealogy of Economy and Government*, translated by Lorenzo Chiesa and Matteo Mandarini. Stanford, CA: Stanford University Press, 2011.

Anderson, Benedict. *Imagined Communities: Reflections on the Origin and Spread of Nationalism*. London: Verso Books, 2006.

Ardener, Edwin. "Witchcraft, Economics, and the Continuity of Belief." In *Witchcraft Confessions and Accusations*, edited by Mary Douglas, 141–160. London: Routledge, 2004.

Aristotle. *History of Animals*. https://el.wikisource.org/wiki/%CE%A4%CF%89%CE%BD_%CF%80%CE%B5%CF%81%CE%AF_%CF%84%CE%B1_%CE%B6%CF%8E%CE%B1_%CE%B9%CF%83%CF%84%CE%BF%CF%81%CE%B9%CF%8E%CE%BD/1.

Arruzza, Cinzia, Tithi Bhattacharya, and Nancy Fraser. *Feminism for the 99%: A Manifesto*. London: Verso, 2019.

Atharva Veda, vol. 1. Edited by Shankar Pandurang Pandit. Bombay: Government Central Book Depot, 1895.

Atharva-Veda Samhita, vol. 1. Edited and translated by William Dwight Whitney and Charles Rockwell Lanman. Cambridge, MA: Harvard University Press, 1905.

Austin, John. *The Province of Jurisprudence Determined*. London: John Murray, 1861.

Banerjee, Abhijit V. and Esther Duflo. *Poor Economics: A Radical Rethinking of the Way to Fight Global Poverty*. New York: Public Affairs, 2012.

Banerjee, Milinda. "Gods in a Democracy: State of Nature, Postcolonial Politics, and Bengali Mangalkabyas." In *The Postcolonial World*, edited by Jyotsna G. Singh and David D. Kim, 184–205. London: Routledge, 2016.

Banerjee, Milinda. "'We shall Create a New World, a New Man, a New Society': Globalized Horizons among Bengali Naxalites." In *The Global 1960s: Convention, Contest, and Counterculture*, edited by Tamara Chaplin and Jadwiga E. Pieper Mooney, 52–71. Abingdon: Routledge, 2018.

Banerjee, Milinda. *The Mortal God. Imagining the Sovereign in Colonial India*. Cambridge: Cambridge University Press, 2018.

Banerjee, Milinda. "A Non-Eurocentric Genealogy of Indian Democracy: Tripura in History of Political Thought." In *Vernacular Politics in Northeast India: Democracy, Ethnicity, and Indigeneity*, edited by Jelle J. P. Wouters, 83–109. Oxford: Oxford University Press, 2022.

Barma, Panchanan. "Letter to the Chief Secretary to the Government of Bengal, 1917." In *Kshatriya Samiti, San 1324 Saler Ashtam Varsher Vrittavivaran*, 50–55. Rangpur: Kshatriya Samiti, 1918.

Baus, Emma. *Animal Democracy* [documentary]. Producer: Cocottes Minute/Arte, 2021.

Bell, Karen. "A Working-Class Green Movement Is Out There but Not Getting the Credit It Deserves." *The Guardian*. 11 October 2019.

Benedict, Ruth. *The Chrysanthemum And The Sword: Patterns of Japanese Culture*. Boston: Houghton Mifflin, 1946.

Bennett, Eric. "How Iowa Flattened Literature". *Chronicle of Higher Education*, 10 February 2014.

Bharata. *Natyashastra*. Edited and translated by Sureshchandra Bandyopadhyay and Chhanda Chakravarti. Calcutta: Navapatra Prakashan, 1956.

Bhattacharya, Tithi, and Sarah Jaffe. "Social Reproduction and the Pandemic." *Dissent*, 2 April 2020. https://www.dissentmagazine.org/online_articles/social-reproduction-and-the-pandemic-with-tithi-bhattacharya.

Biswas, Manohar Mouli. *Amar Bhuvane Ami Bneche Thaki*. Calcutta: Chaturtha Duniya, 2013.

Blaser, Mario. "Political Ontology." *Cultural Studies* 23, no 5-6 (2009): 873–896.

Blaser, Mario. "Is Another Cosmopolitics Possible?" *Cultural Anthropology* 31, no 4 (2016): 545–570.

Chaitanya, "Shikshashtakam." In Krishnadas Kaviraj, *Chaitanyacharitamrita*, edited by Sukumar Sen, 613–16. Delhi: Sahitya Akademi, 1963.

Chakrabarty, Dipesh. *Provincializing Europe: Postcolonial Thought and Historical Difference*. Princeton: Princeton University Press, 2000.

Chakrabarty, Dipesh. *The Climate of History in a Planetary Age*. Chicago: University of Chicago Press, 2021.

Chakravarti, Nirendranath. *Shreshtha Kavita*. Calcutta: Bharavi, 1960.

Chakravorty Spivak, Gayatri. "Can the Subaltern Speak?" In *Marxism and the Interpretation of Culture,* edited by Cary Nelson and Lawrence Grossberg, 271–313. Macmillan Education: Basingstoke, 1988.

Chakravorty Spivak, Gayatri. *Ganatantrer Rahasya*. Calcutta: Anushtup, 2019.

Chakravorty Spivak, Gayatri. *Yukti o Kalpanashakti*. Calcutta: Anushtup, 2020.

Chao, Sophie. *In the Shadow of the Palms: More-Than-Human Becomings in West Papua*. Durham: Duke University Press, 2022.

Chatterjee, Partha. *The Nation and Its Fragments: Colonial and Postcolonial Histories*. Princeton: Princeton University Press, 1993.

Chatterjee, Partha. *Lineages of Political Society: Studies in Postcolonial Democracy*. New York: Columbia University Press, 2011.

Chattopadhyay, Bankimchandra. "Hanumadbabu Samvad." In *Bankim Rachanavali*, vol. 2, 37–40. Calcutta: Sahitya Samsad, 1954.

Chibber, Vivek. *Postcolonial Theory and the Specter of Capital*. London: Verso, 2013.

Clastres, Pierre. *Society against the State: Essays in Political Anthropology*. New York: Zone Books, 1977.

Comaroff, John, L. and Jean Comaroff. *Ethnicity, Inc.* Chicago: University of Chicago Press, 2009.

Combahee River Collective Statement. 1977. https://www.blackpast. org/african-american-history/combahee-river-collective-statement-1977/.

Constitution of Ecuador. 2008. https://pdba.georgetown.edu/ Constitutions/Ecuador/ecuador.html.

Constitution of the Kingdom of Bhutan. 2008. https://www. nationalcouncil.bt/assets/uploads/files/Constitution%20%20 of%20Bhutan%20English.pdf.

Copeland, Shawn. M. *Knowing Christ Crucified: The Witness of African American Religious Experience*. Maryknoll, NY: Orbis Books, 2018.

Cowper, William. *The Solitude of Alexander Selkirk*. https://www. bartleby.com/41/317.html.

Crutzen, Paul J. and Eugene F. Stoermer. "The 'Anthropocene.'" *Global Change Newsletter* 41 (May 2000): 17–18.

Dante, Alighieri. *The Divine Comedy*. https://digitaldante.columbia. edu/dante/divine-comedy/.

Das, Krishnaram. "Raymangal." In *Kavi Krishnaram Daser Granthavali*, edited by Satyanarayan Bhattacharya, 165–248. Calcutta: University of Calcutta Press, 1958.

David-Neel, Alexandra and The Lama Yongden. *The Superhuman Life of Gesar of Ling*. London: Rider and Co., 1933.

De la Cadena, Marisol. *Earth Beings: Ecologies of Practice across Andean Worlds*. Durham: Duke University Press, 2015.

De la Cadena, Marisol and Mario Blaser, eds. *A World of Many Worlds*. Durham: Duke University Press, 2018.

De Maaker, Erik. *Reworking Culture: Relatedness, Rites, and Resources in the Garo Hills, North East India*. Oxford: Oxford University Press, 2022.

214

Deb, Dasarath. *Mukti Parishader Itikatha*. Calcutta: National Book Agency, 1987.

Deleuze, Gilles and Félix Guattari. *A Thousand Plateaus: Capitalism and Schizophrenia*. Translated by Brian Massumi. Minneapolis: University of Minnesota Press, 1987.

Derrida, Jacques. *Of Grammatology*. Translated by Gayatri Chakravorty Spivak. Baltimore: Johns Hopkins University Press, 1976.

Derrida, Jacques. *The Animal that Therefore I Am*. Translated by David Wills. New York: Fordham University Press, 2008.

Descartes, René. *Discours de la méthode*. Paris: Ernest Flammarion, 1908.

Descola, Philippe. *Beyond Nature and Culture*. Translated by Janet Lloyd. Chicago: University of Chicago Press, 2013.

Donaldson, Sue and Will Kymlicka. *Zoopolis: A Political Theory of Animal Rights*. Oxford: Oxford University Press, 2013.

Douglas, Mary, ed. *Witchcraft Confessions and Accusations*. London: Routledge, 2004.

Durkheim, Émile. *The Elementary Forms of Religious Life*. Translated by Karen E. Fields. New York: The Free Press, 1995.

Ecks, Stefan. *Living Worth: Value and Values in Global Pharmaceutical Markets*. Durham: Duke University Press, 2022.

Eggeling, Julius. *The Shatapatha Brahmana*. Delhi: Motilal Banarsidass, 1966.

Escobar, Arturo. *Territories of Difference: Place, Movements, Life, Redes*. Durham: Duke University Press, 2008.

Fausböll, Viggo, ed. "Tittirajataka." In *Jatakatthavannana, vol. 1*, 217–220. London: Trübner & Co., 1877.

Fausböll, Viggo, ed. "Mahasutasomajataka." In *Jatakatthavannana, vol. 5*, 456–511. London: Kegan Paul Trench Trübner & Co., 1891.

Findly, Ellison Banks. *Plant Lives: Borderline Beings in Indian Traditions*. Delhi: Motilal Banarsidass, 2008.

Fisher, Mark. *Capitalist Realism: Is There No Alternative?* London: John Hunt, 2009.

Feuerbach, Ludwig. *The Essence of Christianity*. Translated by Marian Evans. London: John Chapman, 1854.

Foucault, Michel. *Security, Territory, Population: Lectures at the Collège de France, 1977–78*. Translated by Graham Burchell. New York: Palgrave Macmillan, 2007.

Friedman, Milton. *Capitalism and Freedom*. Chicago: Chicago University Press, 1962.

Gago, Verónica. *Feminist International: How to Change Everything*. Translated by Liz Mason-Deese. London: Verso. 2020.

Ghebreyesus, Tedros Adhanom. "I Run the W.H.O., and I Know that Rich Countries Must Make a Choice." *The New York Times*, 22 April 2021. https://www.nytimes.com/2021/04/22/opinion/who-covid-vaccines.html.

Ghosh, Amitav. *The Great Derangement: Climate Change and the Unthinkable*. Chicago: University of Chicago Press, 2016.

Gleeson, Jules Joanne and Nathaniel Dickson. "The Future of Trans Politics." 14 March 2019. https://www.versobooks.com/blogs/4269-the-future-of-trans-politics.

Government of Tripura. *Svadhin Tripura Gramyamandali Ain*. Edited by Bijay Debbarma and Arun Debbarma. Agartala: Government of Tripura, 2006.

Gramsci, Antonio. *Selections from the Prison Notebooks of Antonio Gramsci*. New York: International Publishers, 1971.

Guha, Ranajit, ed. *Subaltern Studies I: Writings on South Asian History and Society*. Delhi: Oxford University Press, 1982.

Guha, Ranajit. *Elementary Aspects of Peasant Insurgency in Colonial India*. Delhi: Oxford University Press, 1983.

Hallowell, A. Irving. *The Ojibwa of Berens River, Manitoba: Ethnography into History*. Fort Worth: Harcourt Brace Jovanovich College Publishers, 1992.

Haraway, Donna, J. *When Species Meet*. Minneapolis: University of Minnesota Press, 2007.

Haraway, Donna J. *Staying with the Trouble: Making Kin in the Chthulucene*. Durham: Duke University Press, 2016.

Hardt, Michael and Antonio Negri. *Empire*. Cambridge, MA: Harvard University Press, 2000.

Hardt, Michael and Antonio Negri. *Assembly*. New York: Oxford University Press, 2017.

Haridev. *Haridever Rachanavali: Raymangal o Shitalamangal*. Edited by Panchanan Mandal. Santiniketan: Viswa-Bharati, 1960.

Haudenosaunee Thanksgiving Address, Greetings to the Natural World. https://americanindian.si.edu/environment/pdf/01_02_Thanksgiving_Address.pdf.

Hayek, Friedrich A. *The Road to Serfdom*. Chicago: University of Chicago Press, 1944.

Hayek, Friedrich A. *The Constitution of Liberty*. Chicago: University of Chicago Press, 1960.

Hedin, Sven. *Trans-Himalaya: Discoveries and Adventures in Tibet*. New York: The Macmillan Company, 1909.

Hegel, Georg Wilhelm Friedrich. *The Philosophy of History*. Translated by J. Sibree. New York: The Colonial Press, 1899.

Hegel, Georg Wilhelm Friedrich. *Phänomenologie des Geistes*. Leipzig: Verlag von Felix Meiner, 1907.

Hegel, Georg Wilhelm Friedrich. *Naturrecht und Staatswissenschaft im Grundrisse: Grundlinien der Philosophie des Rechts.* Leipzig: Verlag von Felix Meiner, 1911.

Hickel, Jason. *Less is More: How Degrowth Will Save the World.* London: Penguin, 2020.

Hobsbawm, Eric J. *Primitive Rebels: Studies in Archaic Forms of Social Movement in the 19th and 20th Centuries.* Manchester: Manchester University Press, 1963.

Horton, Helena. "Octopuses and Lobsters have Feelings — include them in Sentience Bill, urge MPs." *The Guardian.* 18 June 2021. https://www.theguardian.com/world/2021/jun/18/octopuses-and-lobsters-have-feelings-include-them-in-sentience-bill-urge-mps.

Hymns of the Atharva-Veda. Translated by Maurice Bloomfield. Oxford: Clarendon Press, 1897.

I Fioretti di S. Francesco. Edited by Arnaldo della Torre. Turin: G. B. Paravia and Co., 1909.

Ilaiah, Kancha. *Why I am Not a Hindu: A Sudra Critique of Hindutva Philosophy, Culture and Political Economy.* Calcutta: Samya, 1996.

Islam, Kazi Nazrul. "Mora Sabai Svadhin, Mora Sabai Raja." In *Kazi Nazrul Islam Rachanasamagra*, vol. 2, 417–19. Calcutta: Pashchimbanga Bangla Akademi, 2005.

Jamison, Stephanie, W. and Joel P. Brereton, trans. *The Rigveda: The Earliest Religious Poetry of India, vol. 1.* Oxford: Oxford University Press, 2014.

Kalidasa. *Meghaduta.* Edited and translated by Panchkari Ghosh. Chinsurah: Pramathanath Basu, 1938.

Kallis, Giorgos. *Degrowth.* New York: Columbia University Press, 2018.

Kautilya. *Kautilyam Arthashastram.* Edited by R. Shama Sastri. Mysore: Government Branch Press, 1919.

Kautilya. *King, Governance, and Law in Ancient India: Kautilya's Arthasastra.* Translated by Patrick Olivelle. Oxford: Oxford University Press, 2013.

Kimmerer, Robin Wall. *Braiding Sweetgrass: Indigenous Wisdom, Scientific Knowledge, and the Teachings of Plants.* Minneapolis: Milkweed Press, 2015.

Kohn, Eduardo. *How Forests Think: Toward an Anthropology Beyond the Human.* Durham: Duke University Press, 2013.

Kopenawa, Davi and Bruce Albert. *The Falling Sky: Words of a Yanomami Shaman.* Translated by Nicholas Elliott and Alison Dundy. Cambridge, MA: Harvard University Press, 2013.

Kropotkin, Peter. *Mutual Aid: A Factor of Evolution.* London: William Heinemann, 1902.

Latour, Bruno. *Facing Gaia: Eight Lectures on the New Climatic Regime*. Cambridge: Polity Press, 2017.

Law of the Rights of Mother Earth. Bolivia, 2010. http://www.planificacion.gob.bo/uploads/marco-legal/Ley%20N%C2%B0%20071%20DERECHOS%20DE%20LA%20MADRE%20TIERRA.pdf.

Lawrence, D.H. "Snake." https://poets.org/poem/snake-0.

Lee, Richard B., and Irven DeVore, ed. *Kalahari Hunter-Gatherers: Studies of the !Kung San and their Neighbors*. Cambridge, MA: Harvard University Press, 1976.

Lepenies, Philipp. *The Power of a Single Number: A Political History of GDP*. New York: Columbia University Press, 2016.

Locke, John. *Two Treatises of Government*. Cambridge: Cambridge University Press, 1988.

Lowe, Lisa. *The Intimacies of Four Continents*. Durham: Duke University Press, 2015.

Lyotard, Jean-François. *The Postmodern Condition: A Report on Knowledge*. Translated by Geoff Bennington and Brian Massumi. Manchester: Manchester University Press, 1984.

Macpherson, C. B. *The Political Theory of Possessive Individualism: Hobbes to Locke*. Oxford: Oxford University Press, 1962.

Maha Upanishad. https://sanskritdocuments.org/doc_upanishhat/maha.pdf

Malm, Andreas. *Fossil Capital: The Rise of Steam Power and the Roots of Global Warming*. London: Verso, 2016.

Malm, Andreas. "Who Lit This Fire? Approaching the History of the Fossil Economy." *Critical Historical Studies* 3 (2) 2016: 215–48.

Malm, Andreas. *How to Blow Up a Pipeline: Learning to Fight in a World on Fire*. London: Verso, 2021.

Marx, Karl. *Capital: A Critique of Political Economy*, vols. 1-3. https://www.marxists.org/archive/marx/works/1867-c1/, https://www.marxists.org/archive/marx/works/1885-c2/index.htm, and https://www.marxists.org/archive/marx/works/1894-c3/.

Marx, Karl. *The Eighteenth Brumaire of Louis Bonaparte*. Translated by Daniel de Leon. New York: International Publishing Co., 1898.

Marx, Karl. *Critique of Hegel's "Philosophy of Right."* Translated by Annette Jolin and Joseph O' Malley. Cambridge: Cambridge University Press, 2009.

Marx, Karl, and Friedrich Engels. *The Communist Manifesto*. Chicago: Pluto Press, 1996.

Majumdar, Ashutosh. *Meyeder Brata-Katha*. Calcutta: Dev Sahitya Kutir, n.d.

Mauss, Marcel. *The Gift: Forms and Functions of Exchange in Archaic Societies*. London: Cohen & West, 1966.

McBrien, Justin. "Accumulating Extinction: Planetary Catastrophism in the Necrocene." In *Anthropocene or Capitalocene? Nature, History, and the Crisis of Capitalism*, edited by Jason W. Moore, 116–137. Oakland, CA: PM Press.

"Merkel Says Vaccine Patent Waiver 'Not the Solution' — as It Happened." *The Guardian*. May 8, 2021. https://www.theguardian.com/world/live/2021/may/08/coronavirus-live-news-india-lockdown-uk-covid-19-vaccines.

Moore, Jason W. *Capitalism in the Web of Life: Ecology and the Accumulation of Capital*. London: Verso, 2015.

Moore, Jason W., ed. *Anthropocene or Capitalocene? Nature, History, and the Crisis of Capitalism*. Oakland, CA: PM Press, 2016.

Moyle, J. B., trans. *The Institutes of Justinian*. Oxford: Clarendon Press, 1889.

Mukerji, Dhan Gopal. *The Chief of the Herd*. London: J. M. Dent and Sons, 1929.

Mukunda. *Chandimangal*. Edited by Sukumar Sen. Calcutta: Sahitya Akademi, 1955.

Olivelle, Patrick, trans. *The Pancatantra: The Book of India's Folk Wisdom*. Oxford: Oxford University Press, 1997.

Olivelle, Patrick. *The Early Upanisads: Annotated Text and Translation*. New York: Oxford University Press, 1998.

Olivelle, Patrick, trans. *Dharmasutras: The Law Codes of Apastamba, Gautama, Baudhayana, and Vasistha*. Oxford: Oxford University Press, 1999.

Olivelle, Patrick, trans. *Manu's Code of Law*. Oxford: Oxford University Press, 2005.

Olsen, Niklas. *The Sovereign Consumer: A New Intellectual History of Neoliberalism*. Cham: Palgrave Macmillan, 2019.

Ortner, Sherry B. "Dark Anthropology and Its Others: Theory since the eighties." *HAU: Journal of Ethnographic Theory* 6, no 1 (2016): 47–73.

Phizo, "Plebiscite Speech." 1951. https://www.neuenhofer.de/guenter/nagaland/phizo.html.

Phule, Jotirao Govindrao. *Slavery: In the Civilised British Government Under the Cloak of Brahmanism*. Translated by P.G. Patil. Bombay: Education Department, Government of Maharashtra, 1991.

Phuntsho, Karma. *The History of Bhutan*. New Delhi: Random House, 2013.

Piketty, Thomas. *Capital in the Twenty-First Century*. Translated by Arthur Goldhammer. Cambridge, MA: Harvard University Press, 2014.

Piketty, Thomas. *Capital and Ideology*. Translated by Arthur Goldhammer. Cambridge, MA: Harvard University Press, 2020.

Piketty, Thomas. "The G7 Legalizes the Right to Defraud." 15 June 2021. https://www.lemonde.fr/blog/piketty/2021/06/15/the-g7-legalizes-the-right-to-defraud/.

Plato. *Phaedo.* http://www.perseus.tufts.edu/hopper/text?doc=Perseus%3atext%3a1999.01.0169%3atext%3dPhaedo.

Plutarch. *De sollertia animalium.* http://www.perseus.tufts.edu/hopper/text?doc=Perseus%3Atext%3A2008.01.0368.

Polybius. *Histories.* http://www.perseus.tufts.edu/hopper/text?doc=Perseus%3atext%3a1999.01.0233.

Postone, Moishe. *Time, Labor, and Social Domination: A Reinterpretation of Marx's Critical Theory.* Cambridge: Cambridge University Press, 1993.

Riofrancos, Thea. *Resource Radicals: From Petro-Nationalism to Post-Extractivism in Ecuador.* Durham: Duke University Press, 2020.

Robbins, Joel. "Beyond the Suffering Subject: Toward an Anthropology of the Good." *Journal of the Royal Anthropological Institute* 19, no 3 (September, 2013): 447–462.

Rosa-Aquino, Paola. "Animals Vote, Too: How Different Species Choose — or Depose — a Leader." *The Guardian.* 3 November 2020. https://www.theguardian.com/environment/2020/nov/03/animal-democracy-bees-ants-pigeons-choose-leader.

Rose, Hilary, and Steven Rose. *Genes, Cells and Brains: The Promethean Promises of the New Biology.* London: Verso, 2014.

Roy, Anupam. "Manush Bhalo Nei." https://www.youtube.com/watch?v=DAGwJBsh5CE.

Roychowdhury, Upendra Kishore. "Majantali Sarkar." In *Tuntunir Boi,* 113–19. Calcutta: Dev Sahitya Kutir, 1964.

Sahlins, Marshall D. "Poor Man, Rich Man, Big-Man, Chief: Political Types in Melanesia and Polynesia." *Comparative Studies in Society and History* 5, no 3 (April 1963): 285–303.

Sahlins, Marshall. "The Stranger-King or, Elementary Forms of the Politics of Life." *Indonesia and the Malay World* 36, no. 105 (September, 2008): 177–199.

Sahlins, Marshall. "The Original Political Society." *HAU: Journal of Ethnographic Theory* 7, no 2 (2017): 91–128.

Sarkar, Sumit. *Writing Social History.* Delhi: Oxford University Press, 1997.

Sartori, Andrew. *Liberalism in Empire: An Alternative History.* Oakland: University of California Press, 2014.

Schmitt, Carl. *The Concept of the Political.* Translated by George Schwab. Chicago: Chicago University Press, 2007.

Scott, James C. *The Art of Not Being Governed: An Anarchist History of Upland Southeast Asia.* New Haven: Yale University Press, 2009.

Scott, James C. *Against the Grain: A Deep History of the Earliest States*. New Haven: Yale University Press, 2017.

Sen, Kaliprasanna, ed. *Shrirajmala, vols. 1–4*. Agartala: Government of Tripura, 2003.

Sen, Kshitimohan, ed. and trans. *Kabir, vols. 1–4*. Calcutta: Indian Publishing House, 1910–11.

Shatapatha Brahmana. http://gretil.sub.uni-goettingen.de/gretil/1_sanskr/1_veda/2_bra/satapath/sb_01_u.htm.

Shatapatha Brahmana, Part II. Translated by Julius Eggeling. Oxford: Clarendon Press, 1885.

Sheldrake, Merlin. *Entangled Life: How Fungi Make Our Worlds, Change Our Minds & Shape Our Futures*. London: Random House, 2020.

Skotnes-Brown, Jules. "Domestication, Degeneration, and the Establishment of the Addo Elephant National Park in South Africa, 1910s–1930s." *The Historical Journal* 64, no 2 (2021): 357–383.

Smith, Brian K. *Classifying the Universe: The Ancient Indian Varna System and the Origins of Caste*. Oxford: Oxford University Press, 1994.

Sohn-Rethel, Alfred. *Intellectual and Manual Labour: A Critique of Epistemology*. Translated by Martin Sohn-Rethel. Leiden: Brill, 2021.

Spade, Dean. *Mutual Aid: Building Solidarity During this Crisis (and the Next)*. London: Verso, 2020.

Stern, Philip J. *The Company-State: Corporate Sovereignty and the Early Modern Foundations of the British Empire in India*. Oxford: Oxford University Press, 2011.

Tagore, Abanindranath. *Banglar Brata*. Calcutta: Viswa-Bharati, 1943.

Tagore, Abanindranath. *Buro Angla*. Calcutta: Signet Press, 1953.

Tagore, Rabindranath. "Aj Dhaner Kshete." https://www.geetabitan.com/lyrics/A/aaj-dhaaner-khete-roudro-lyric.html.

Tagore, Rabindranath. "Hathat Dekha." https://www.kobikolpolota.in/hothat-dekha-kobita-poem/.

Tagore, Rabindranath. "The Message of the Forest." In *The English Writings of Rabindranath Tagore*, vol. 3, edited by Sisir Kumar Das, 385–400. Delhi: Sahitya Akademi, 1996.

Taussig, Michael T. *The Devil and Commodity Fetishism in South America*. Chapel Hill: University Of North Carolina Press, 1980.

Te Awa Tupua (Whanganui River Claims Settlement) Act. 2017. https://www.legislation.govt.nz/act/public/2017/0007/latest/whole.html.

Thakur Charal, Kalyani. *Ami Keno Charal Likhi*. Calcutta: Chaturtha Duniya, 2016.

Tsing, Anna Lowenhaupt. *The Mushroom at the End of the World: On the Possibility of Life in Capitalist Ruins*. Princeton: Princeton University Press, 2015.

Universal Declaration of the Rights of Mother Earth. 2010. https://pwccc.wordpress.com/programa/.

Ura, Karma. "Deities and Environment." 2001. https://lib.icimod.org/record/10801/files/117.pdf.

Vaidya, P. L., ed. *Lalitavistara*. Darbhanga: The Mithila Institute of Post-Graduate Studies and Research in Sanskrit Learning, 1958.

Van Dooren, Thom. *Vulture*. London: Reaktion Books, 2011.

Van Dooren, Thom. *Flight Ways: Life and Loss at the Edge of Extinction*. New York: Columbia University Press, 2014.

Van Dooren, Thom. *The Wake of Crows: Living and Dying in Shared Worlds*. New York: Columbia University Press, 2019.

Varro. *De re rustica*. http://penelope.uchicago.edu/Thayer/E/Roman/Texts/Varro/de_Re_Rustica/home.html.

Vergès, Françoise. *A Decolonial Feminism*. Translated by Ashley J. Bohrer. London: Pluto, 2021.

Virgil. *Aeneid*. https://www.perseus.tufts.edu/hopper/text?doc=Perseus:text:1999.02.0055.

Virgil. *Georgics*. http://www.perseus.tufts.edu/hopper/text?doc=Perseus:text:1999.02.0059.

Viswanathan, Gauri. *Masks of Conquest: Literary Study and British Rule in India*. New York: Columbia University Press, 2014.

Viveiros de Castro, Eduardo. "Cosmological Deixis and Amerindian Perspectivism." *The Journal of the Royal Anthropological Institute* 4, no 3 (September 1998): 469–488.

Viveiros de Castro, Eduardo. *The Relative Native: Essays on Indigenous Conceptual Worlds*. Chicago: HAU Books, 2015.

Von Fürer-Haimendorf, Christoph. *Return to the Naked Nagas: An Anthropologist's View of Nagaland, 1936–1970*. London: John Murray, 1976.

Vuković, Krešimir. *Wolves of Rome: The Lupercalia from Roman and Comparative Perspectives*. Berlin: De Gruyter, 2022.

Vyasa. *Mahabharata*. http://gretil.sub.uni-goettingen.de/gretil/1_sanskr/2_epic/mbh/sas/mahabharata.htm.

Wangdi, Rinzin and Michaela Windischgraetz. "The Black-Slate Edict of Punakha Dzong." *Bhutan Law Network/JSW Law Research Paper Series No. 20-02* (2019): 1–60.

Watkins, Calvert, ed. *The American Heritage Dictionary of Indo-European Roots*. Boston: Houghton Mifflin Company, 1985.

Weber, Albrecht. *Indische Studien*. Leipzig: F. A. Brockhaus, 1898.

Whitehead, Hal and Luke Rendell. *The Cultural Lives of Whales and Dolphins*. Chicago: University of Chicago Press, 2014.

Witzel, Michael. "Early Sanskritization: Origins and Development of the Kuru State." *Electronic Journal of Vedic Studies* 1-4 (1995): 1-26.

World Health Organization. "Mental Health." 2021. https://www.who.int/health-topics/mental-health#tab=tab_2

World Wildlife Fund. "Living Planet Report 2018." 2018. https://www.worldwildlife.org/pages/living-planet-report-2018/.

Wouters, Jelle J.P. "Nagas as a 'Society Against Voting?' Consensus-Building, Party-less Politics, and a Culturalist Critique of Elections in Northeast India." *The Cambridge Journal of Anthropology* 36, no. 2 (Autumn 2018): 113-132.

Wouters, Jelle J.P. *In the Shadows of Naga Insurgency: Tribes, State, and Violence in Northeast India.* New Delhi: Oxford University Press, 2018.

Yelle, Robert A. *Sovereignty and the Sacred: Secularism and the Political Economy of Religion.* Chicago: University Of Chicago Press, 2018.

Yengde, Suraj. *Caste Matters.* New Delhi: Penguin Viking, 2019.

Zuboff, Shoshana. *The Age of Surveillance Capitalism: The Fight for a Human Future at the New Frontier of Power.* New York: Public Affairs, 2019.

Also available from Prickly Paradigm Press: